How to Read the New Testament
Book by Book

Also by Gordon D. Fee and Douglas Stuart

How to Read the Bible for All Its Worth

Also by Gordon D. Fee and Mark L. Strauss

How to Choose a Translation for All Its Worth

How to Read the New Testament Book by Book *A Guided Tour*

Gordon D. Fee
Douglas Stuart

**ZONDERVAN
ACADEMIC**

ZONDERVAN ACADEMIC

How to Read the New Testament Book by Book
Copyright © 2002, 2023 by Gordon D. Fee and Douglas Stuart

The content of this book is also published in *How to Read the Bible Book by Book*.

Requests for information should be addressed to:
Zondervan, 3900 *Sparks Dr. SE, Grand Rapids, Michigan 49546*

Zondervan titles may be purchased in bulk for educational, business, fundraising, or sales promotional use. For information, please email SpecialMarkets@Zondervan.com.

ISBN 978-0-310-15591-1 (softcover)
ISBN 978-0-310-15599-7 (audio)
ISBN 978-0-310-15594-2 (ebook)

Cover design: *Rob Monacelli*
Cover photo: *©Pixel-Shot / Shutterstock*
Interior design: *Nancy Wilson*

Printed in the United States of America

23 24 25 26 27 LBC 5 4 3 2 1

For Walker, Maia, and Emma
Joshua, Julia, Cherisa, Nathan, and Benjamin
Zachary and Jackson
Maricel and Annalise
and
Meriwether and Honour
and Mcaela
that they may learn to read the Story well
and love Him whose Story it is
(Psalm 71:14–18; Psalm 103:17)

ABBREVIATIONS

OLD TESTAMENT

Gen	Genesis	Song	Song of Songs
Exod	Exodus	Isa	Isaiah
Lev	Leviticus	Jer	Jeremiah
Num	Numbers	Lam	Lamentations
Deut	Deuteronomy	Ezek	Ezekiel
Josh	Joshua	Dan	Daniel
Judg	Judges	Hos	Hosea
Ruth	Ruth	Joel	Joel
1–2 Sam	1–2 Samuel	Amos	Amos
1–2 Kgs	1–2 Kings	Obad	Obadiah
1–2 Chr	1–2 Chronicles	Jonah	Jonah
Ezra	Ezra	Mic	Micah
Neh	Nehemiah	Nah	Nahum
Esth	Esther	Hab	Habakkuk
Job	Job	Zeph	Zephaniah
Ps/Pss	Psalms	Hag	Haggai
Prov	Proverbs	Zech	Zechariah
Eccl	Ecclesiastes	Mal	Malachi

NEW TESTAMENT

Matt	Matthew	1–2 Thess	1–2 Thessalonians
Mark	Mark	1–2 Tim	1–2 Timothy
Luke	Luke	Titus	Titus
John	John	Phlm	Philemon
Acts	Acts	Heb	Hebrews
Rom	Romans	Jas	James
1–2 Cor	1–2 Corinthians	1–2 Pet	1–2 Peter
Gal	Galatians	1–2–3 John	1–2–3 John
Eph	Ephesians	Jude	Jude
Phil	Philippians	Rev	Revelation
Col	Colossians		

A.D.	*anno Domini* (in the year of [our] Lord)	f(f).	and the following one(s)
B.C.	before Christ	i.e.	*id est,* that is
ca.	*circa,* about, approximately	lit.	literally
cf.	*confer,* compare	NT	New Testament
ch(s).	chapter(s)	OT	Old Testament
e.g.	*exempli gratia,* for example	p(p).	page(s)
esp.	especially	par.	parallel (textual parallels)
et al.	*et alii,* and others	v(v).	verse(s)
etc.	*et cetera,* and the rest	*x*	number of times a form occurs

Contents

Preface 9

The Biblical Story: An Overview. 14

THE GOSPELS AND ACTS
IN THE BIBLICAL STORY ■ 21

Matthew 23   Acts 50

Mark 31   John 58

Luke 40

THE EPISTLES AND REVELATION
IN THE BIBLICAL STORY ■ 69

Romans 71   Titus 137

1 Corinthians 78   Philemon 141

2 Corinthians 87   Hebrews 144

Galatians 94   James 151

Ephesians 101   1 Peter 156

Philippians 107   2 Peter 161

Colossians 113   1 John 165

1 Thessalonians 118   2 John 171

2 Thessalonians 123   3 John 174

1 Timothy 127   Jude 177

2 Timothy 133   The Revelation 180

Glossary of Terms 191

Appendix: A Chronological Listing of the Biblical Books 197

Preface

This book is intended to be a companion to *How to Read the Bible for All Its Worth*. That book was designed to help people become better readers of Scripture by taking into account the various kinds of literature that make up the Christian Bible. Through an understanding of how the various types "work," how they differ from one another, and how they raise different kinds of hermeneutical questions, we hoped that one might learn to read the Bible in a more informed way.

The success of that first book has given us the courage to try another. The aim is still the same: to help people become better *readers* of Scripture. What we hope to do here is to go a step beyond the first book: Assuming the principles of the first book, here we try to help you read—and understand—each of the biblical books on its own but especially to help you see how each one fits with the others to form the great narrative of Scripture.

But this book has undergone its own form of evolution. Some years ago we were asked to write a Bible survey textbook of the kind that many students have been exposed to over the years. For a variety of reasons, but mostly because we could never get our hearts into it, that project simply did not work out. To be sure, we hope this book will still serve the purposes of survey courses, but we have intentionally tried to write something quite different. These differences, as we perceive them, are several.

First, our goal is not simply to dispense knowledge about the various books of the Bible—the kind of knowledge that allows one to pass Bible knowledge exams without ever reading the Bible! Such books and exams usually deal with a lot of data but very often with little sense of how the various books of the Bible function as entities on their own or of how each fits into *God's story*. Our present concern is almost altogether with the latter. And in any case, the concern is with your becoming a better *reader* of Scripture; if you begin to learn some other things about each book along the way, all the better.

Second, we want to show how the separate entities—each biblical book—fit together as a whole to tell God's story. So much is this a concern that our book is introduced with a brief overview of the biblical story—what those who study narratives call the *metanarrative* of Scripture. This is the big picture, the primary story, of which all the others form a part so as to shape the whole.

Third, in coming to the various biblical books, one by one, we follow a generally consistent format that isolates questions of introduction at the beginning as "Orienting Data for . . ." These kinds of issues (authorship, date, recipients, occasion, and the like) take up much of the space in most surveys. For these (sometimes important) matters there are several surveys, introductions, and Bible dictionaries for both the Old and New Testaments that you may consult. But these matters are often debatable and therefore consume a lot of time that is not always immediately relevant to the reading of the biblical text in its larger setting. Thus, we simply offer some options, or note the traditional view, or settle on one as the perspective from which this guide is written.

But a further word is needed about the matter of authorship, especially for the Old Testament books, since authors in that period did not normally attach their names to what they wrote (with the exception of letters—and there are none of these as books in the Old Testament). When individuals speak about themselves within a given book (e.g., Moses, Nehemiah, Qohelet ["Teacher" in Ecclesiastes]), we may learn something about probable or possible authorship that we wouldn't otherwise know. But for the most part, modern concerns about matters of date and authorship were not given the same attention in ancient Israel; this is made obvious by their absence from most of these books. Many books (e.g., nearly all the historical and poetical books) are entirely anonymous. And even though the source of the content of some books is given—by way of an editorial title at the beginning—and assumptions can often be made that the source also functioned as author, the concern over the book's actual author is not prominent in the book itself. As to dating, just four books—Ezekiel, Daniel, Zechariah, and Haggai—date any of their material, and of those only Haggai does so consistently. Thus we have chosen to minimize authorship in this *reading* guide, leaving it entirely alone when the biblical book itself is anonymous (one can say "unknown" only so many times!). Our interest is in your reading the biblical document in its final canonical form, not in debating the issues of dates, sources, and authorship.

Most of our energy, therefore, has gone into the three major sections of each chapter. The first, "Overview of . . . ," is designed to get you into the book by giving you a sense of what the whole is about. In some ways it is a brief elaboration of the "Content" sentence(s) in the "Orienting" section. The second, "Specific Advice for Reading ... ," tends to elaborate the "Emphases" from the "Orienting" section. Here we offer a way of reading the text, some key themes to keep in mind as you do, or some crucial background material—all of which are designed to help you as you read the text for yourself. The final section, "A Walk through ... ," then takes you by the hand, as it were, and walks you through the book, showing how its various parts work together to form the whole. Sometimes this takes more of an outline form; at other times, because we have purposely tried to keep our chapters brief, you will walk with giant steps. The books of Psalms and Proverbs were understandably the most difficult to fit into this pattern; yet even here we have tried to help you see how the collections are put together.

Above all, we have tried to write a book about the books of the Bible that will not be a substitute for reading the Bible itself. Rather, we hope it may create a desire in you to read each of the biblical books for yourself, while helping you make a fair amount of sense out of what you are reading.

NOTE WELL: The key to using this book is for you to read the first three sections of each chapter ("Orienting Data," "Overview," "Specific Advice"), and then *to read the biblical text* in conjunction with the section titled "A Walk through ... ." If you read "A Walk through" on its own, it will become just more data for you to assimilate. Our intent is for you first to have some important preliminary data in hand, then truly to walk with you through your reading of the biblical book. This will, of course, be far more difficult for some of the longer books, just as it was for us to condense so much material into the brief parameters we allowed ourselves. But even here, while you may be reading over a more extended time period, we hope you will find this a helpful guide. A glossary is provided for those who need some guidance through the maze of technical terms that biblical scholars tend to use without forethought (see p. 191). We have also supplied a suggested chronological listing of the books for those who wish to read them in that order (see the appendix at the back of the book, p. 197).

We have tried to write in such a way that you will be able to follow what is said, no matter which English translation you are using, provided it is a contemporary one (see ch. 2 of *How to Read the Bible for*

All Its Worth). For the New Testament, Professor Fee regularly had Today's New International Version (TNIV) in front of him as he wrote; for the Old Testament, the New International Version (1984 edition) was used. Typically, when Bible verses are cited in this book, they are taken either from the NIV or from the New Testament edition of the TNIV.

A couple of words about presuppositions. First, while we have not assumed that the reader will already have read *How to Read the Bible for All Its Worth,* we do refer to it from time to time (as *How to 1,* with page numbers always referring to the third edition [2003] so that we don't have to repeat some presuppositional things from that book (for example, sources of the Gospels). In the case of Acts and Revelation, which received individual chapters in *How to 1,* that material is reset for this book, but one will still be helped by reading those chapters as well.

Second, the authors unapologetically stand within the evangelical tradition of the church. This means, among other things, that we believe that the Holy Spirit has inspired the biblical writers (and collectors) in their task—even though most often we speak of each document in terms of what the (inspired) human author is doing.

At the same time, in most cases we have tried to be apprised of and make use of the most recent biblical scholarship—although any scholar who might venture to look at this work may well wonder whether we have consulted her or his latest work. Along with our own reading of the text, we herewith gratefully acknowledge that we have incorporated suggestions—and even language—from others too many to mention by name. Those who might recognize some of their ideas in what we have written may, we hope, take pleasure in such recognition; we trust they will also be generous to us when we have chosen to go our own way rather than to be beholden to any other scholarly endeavor.

The authors with gratitude also acknowledge the following: Regent College, whose generous sabbatical policy made it possible for Professor Fee to work on the book during spring term 1998 and winter term 2001; colleagues and friends who have read selected chapters and offered many helpful comments: Iain Provan, V. Philips Long, Rikk Watts, John Stek, Bruce Waltke, and Wendy Wilcox Glidden. Professor Fee's wife, Maudine, has taken great interest in this project by reading every word and making scores of insightful suggestions that have made it a better book. And during the month of March 2001, when Professor Fee was recuperating from surgery, she joined him in reading the entire manuscript and the entire Bible aloud—resulting in scores of changes to the book, as our ears often heard better than our eyes saw. We cannot recommend strongly enough the value of the oral reading of the Bible!

We dedicated *How to 1* to our parents, three of whom have now passed on to be with their Lord. We dedicate this present endeavor to our grandchildren—as of this writing, twelve for the Fees, the oldest of whom are now teenagers, and three for the Stuarts. Thus, in some measure, this book is our own reflection on Psalm 71:14–18.

The Biblical Story:
An Overview

When the authors were boys growing up in Christian homes, one of the ways we—and our friends—were exposed to the Bible was through the daily reading of a biblical text from the Promise Box, which dutifully found its way onto our kitchen tables. Furthermore, most believers of our generation—and of several preceding ones—had learned a kind of devotional reading of the Bible that emphasized reading it only in parts and pieces, looking for a "word for the day."

While the thought behind these approaches to Scripture was salutary enough (constant exposure to the sure promises of God's Word), they also had their downside, teaching people to read texts in a way that disconnected them from the grand story of the Bible.

The concern of this book is to help you read the Bible as a whole, and even when the "whole" is narrowed to "whole books," it is important for you always to be aware of how each book fits into the larger story (on this matter, see *How to 1*, pp. 91–92). But in order to do this, you need first to have a sense of what the grand story is all about. That is what this introduction proposes to do.

First, let's be clear: The Bible is not merely some divine guidebook, nor is it a mine of propositions to be believed or a long list of commands to be obeyed. True, one does receive plenty of guidance from it, and it does indeed contain plenty of true propositions and divine directives. But the Bible is infinitely more than that.

It is no accident that the Bible comes to us primarily by way of narrative—but not just any narrative. Here we have the grandest narrative of all—God's own story. That is, it does not purport to be just one more story of humankind's search for God. No, this is *God's* story, the account of *his* search for us, a story essentially told in four chapters: Creation, Fall, Redemption, Consummation. In this story, God is the divine protagonist, Satan the antagonist, God's people the agonists (although too often also the antagonists), with redemption and reconciliation as the plot resolution.

CREATION

Since this is *God's story,* it does not begin, as do all other such stories, with a hidden God, whom people are seeking and to whom Jesus ultimately leads them. On the contrary, the biblical narrative begins with God as Creator of all that is. It tells us that "in the beginning God ...": that God is *before* all things, that he is the *cause* of all things, that he is therefore *above* all things, and that he is the *goal* of all things. He stands at the origin of all things as the sole cause of the whole universe, in all of its vastness and intricacies. And all creation—all history itself—has the eternal God, through Christ, as its final purpose and consummation.

We are further told that humanity is the crowning glory of the Creator's work—beings made in God's own likeness, with whom he could commune, and in whom he could delight; beings who would know the sheer pleasure of his presence, love, and favor. Created in God's *image,* humankind thus uniquely enjoyed the *vision* of God and lived in *fellowship* with God. We were nonetheless *created* beings and were thus intended to be dependent on the Creator for life and existence in the world. This part of the story is narrated in Genesis 1–2, but it is repeated or echoed in scores of ways throughout the whole narrative.

FALL

The second chapter in the biblical story is a long and tragic one. It begins in Genesis 3, and the dark thread runs through the whole story almost to the very end (Rev 22:11, 15). This "chapter" tells us that man and woman coveted more godlikeness and that in one awful moment in the history of our planet they chose godlikeness over against mere creatureliness, with its dependent status. They chose *in*dependence from the Creator. But we were not intended to live so, and the result was a fall—a colossal and tragic fall. (To be sure, this is not a popular part of the story today, but its rejection is part of the Fall itself and the beginning of all false theologies.)

Made to enjoy God and to be dependent on him, and to find our meaning ultimately in our very creatureliness, we now came under God's wrath and thus came to experience the terrible consequences of our rebellion. The calamity of our fallenness is threefold:

First, we lost our *vision* of God with regard to his nature and character. Guilty and hostile ourselves, we projected that guilt and hostility onto God. God is to blame: "Why have *you* made me thus?" "Why are *you* so cruel?" are the plaintive cries that run throughout the history of our race. We thus became idolaters, now creating gods in our own image; every grotesque expression of our fallenness was reconstructed into a god. Paul puts it this way: "Although they claimed to be wise, they became fools and exchanged the glory of the immortal God for images made to look like mortal human beings and birds and animals and reptiles... They exchanged the truth about God for a lie, and worshiped and served created things rather than the Creator—who is forever praised" (Rom 1:22, 24–25).

In exchanging the truth about God for a lie, we saw God as full of caprice, contradictions, hostility, lust, and retribution (all projections of our fallen selves). But God is *not* like our grotesque idolatries. Indeed, if he is hidden, Paul says, it is because we had become slaves to the god of this world, who has blinded our minds, so that we are ever seeking but never able to find him (see 2 Cor 4:4).

Second, the Fall also caused us to distort—and blur—the *divine image* in ourselves, rolling it in the dust, as it were. Instead of being loving, generous, self-giving, thoughtful, merciful—as God is—we became miserly, selfish, unloving, unforgiving, spiteful. Created to image, and thus represent, God in all that we are and do, we learned rather to bear the image of the Evil One, God's implacable enemy.

The third consequence of the Fall was our loss of the *divine presence* and with that our relationship—fellowship—with God. In place of communion with the Creator, having purpose in his creation, we became rebels, lost and cast adrift, creatures who broke God's laws, abused his creation, and suffered the awful consequences of fallenness in our brokenness, alienation, loneliness, and pain.

Under the tyranny of our sin—indeed, we are enslaved to it, Paul says, and guilty—we found ourselves unwilling and unable to come to the living God for life and restoration. And in turn we passed on our brokenness in the form of every kind of broken relationship with one another (this is writ large in Genesis 4–11).

The Bible tells us that we are fallen, that there is an awful distance between ourselves and God, and that we are like sheep going astray (Isa 53:6; 1 Pet 2:25) or like a rebellious, know-it-all son, living in a far country among the hogs, wanting to eat their food (Luke 15:11–32). In our better moments, we also know that this is the truth not only about the murderer or rapist or child abuser, but also about ourselves—the selfish, the greedy, the proud. It is no wonder people think God is hostile to us; in our better moments we know we deserve his wrath for the kind of endless stinkers we really are.

REDEMPTION

The Bible also tells us that the holy and just God, whose moral perfections burn against sin and creaturely rebellion, is in fact also a God full of mercy and love—and faithfulness. The reality is that God pitied—and loved—these creatures of his, whose rebellion and rejection of their dependent status had caused them to fall so low and thus to experience the pain, guilt, and alienation of their sinfulness.

But how to get through to us, to rescue us from ourselves with all of our wrong views about God and the despair of our tragic fallenness; how to get us to see that God is *for* us, not *against* us (see Rom 8:31); how to get the rebel not just to run up a white flag of surrender but willingly to change sides and thereby once again to discover joy and meaningfulness—that's what chapter 3 of the story is all about.

And it's the longest chapter, a chapter that tells how God set about redeeming and restoring these fallen creatures of his so that he might restore to us the lost vision of God, renew in us the divine image, and reestablish our relationship with him. But also woven throughout this chapter is that other thread—the one of our continuing resistance.

Thus we are told that God came to a man, Abraham, and made a covenant with him—to bless him and, through him, the nations (Genesis 12–50)—and with his offspring, Israel, who had become a slave people (Exodus). Through the first of his prophets, Moses, God (now known by his name *Yahweh*) freed them from their slavery and made a covenant with them at Mount Sinai—that he who had rescued them would be their Savior and Protector forever, that he would be uniquely present with them among all the peoples of the world. But they would also have to keep covenant with him, by letting themselves be reshaped into his likeness. Thus he gave them the Law as his gift to them, both to reveal what he is like and to protect them from one another while they were being reshaped (Leviticus–Deuteronomy).

But the story tells us they rebelled over and over again and looked on his gift of law as a form of taking away their freedom. As shepherds who were being brought into an agricultural land (Joshua), they were not sure their God—a God of shepherds, as they supposed—would also help the

17

crops to grow, so they turned to the agricultural fertility gods (Baal and Ashtoreth) of the peoples who surrounded them.

So they experienced several rounds of oppression and rescue (Judges), even while some of them were truly taking on God's character (Ruth). Finally, God sent them another great prophet (Samuel), who anointed for them their ideal king (David), with whom God made another covenant, specifying that one of his offspring would rule over his people forever (1–2 Samuel). But alas, it goes bad again (1–2 Kings; 1–2 Chronicles), and God in love sends them prophets (Isaiah–Malachi), singers (Psalms), and sages (Job; Proverbs; Ecclesiastes). In the end their constant unfaithfulness is too much, so God at last judges his people with the curses promised in Leviticus 26 and Deuteronomy 28. Yet even here (see Deut 30) there is promise for the future (see, e.g., Isa 40–55; Jer 30–32; Ezek 36–37) in which there would be a new "son of David" and an outpouring of God's Spirit into people's hearts so that they would come to life and be transformed into God's likeness. This final blessing would also include people from all the nations ("the Gentiles").

Finally, just before the last scene, with its final curtain and epilogue, we are told of the greatest event of all—that the great, final "son of David" is none other than God himself, the Creator of all the cosmic greatness and grandeur, come to be present on the human scene in our own likeness. Born as the child of a peasant girl, within the fold of an oppressed people, Jesus the Son of God lived and taught among them. And finally with a horrible death, followed by a death-defeating resurrection, he grappled with and defeated the "gods"—all the powers that have stood against us—and himself bore the full weight of the guilt and punishment of the creatures' rebellion.

Here is the heart of the story: A loving, redeeming God in his incarnation restored our lost *vision* of God (took off the wraps, as it were, so that we could plainly see what God is truly like), by his crucifixion and resurrection made possible our being restored to the *image* of God (see Rom 8:29; 2 Cor 3:18), and through the gift of the Spirit became *present* with us in constant fellowship. Marvelous—well nigh incredible—that revelation, that redemption.

The genius of the biblical story is what it tells us about God himself: a God who sacrifices himself in death out of love for his enemies; a God who would rather experience the death we deserved than to be apart from the people he created for his pleasure; a God who himself bore our likeness, experienced our creatureliness, and carried our sins so that he might provide pardon and reconciliation; a God who would not let us go, but who would pursue us—all of us, even the worst of us—so that he might restore us into joyful fellowship with himself; a God who in Christ Jesus has so forever identified with his beloved creatures that he came to be known and praised as "the God and Father of our Lord Jesus Christ" (1 Pet 1:3).

This is *God's* story, the story of his unfathomable love and grace, mercy and forgiveness—and that is how it also becomes *our* story. The story tells us that we deserve nothing but get everything; that we deserve hell but get heaven; that we deserve to be wiped out, obliterated, but we get his tender embrace; that we deserve rejection and judgment but get to become his children, to bear his likeness, to call him Father. This is the story of the Bible, *God's story,* which at the same time is also our own. Indeed, he even let his human creatures have a part in writing it!

CONSUMMATION

Because the story has not yet ended, the final chapter is still being written—even though we know from what has been written how the final chapter turns out. What God has already set in motion, we are told, through the incarnation, death, and resurrection of Jesus Christ and the gift of the Holy Spirit is finally going to be fully realized.

Thus the one thing that makes this story so different from all other such stories is that ours is filled with hope. There is an End—a glorious conclusion to the present story. It is Jesus, standing at the tomb of his friend Lazarus, telling Lazarus's sister Martha that Jesus himself was her hope for life now and for the life to come: "I am the resurrection and the life," he told her, "anyone who believes in me will live, even though they die"—because Jesus is the *resurrection.* And because he is also the *life,* he went on: "and whoever lives and believes in me will never die" (John 11:25–26). And then he proceeded to validate what he had said by raising Lazarus from the grave.

Jesus himself became the final verification of those words by his own resurrection from the dead. The wicked and the religious killed him. They could not tolerate his presence among them, because he stood in utter contradiction to all their petty forms of religion and authority, based on their own fallenness—and he then had the gall to tell them that he was the *only* way to the Father (see John 14:6). So they killed him. But since he himself *was* Life—and the author of life for all others—the grave couldn't hold him. And his resurrection not only validated his own claims and vindicated his own life on our planet, it also spelled the beginning of the end for death itself and became the guarantee of those who are his—both now and forever.

This is what the final episode (the Revelation) is all about—God's final wrap-up of the story, when his justice brings an end to the great Antagonist and all who continue to bear his image (see Rev 20) and when God in love restores the creation (Eden) as a new heaven and a new earth (see Rev 21–22).

This, then, is the metanarrative, the grand story, of which the various books of the Bible are a part. While we have regularly tried to point out how each book fits in, as you read the various books, you will want to think for yourself how they fit into the larger story. We hope you will also ask yourself how you fit into it as well.

The Gospels
and Acts
in the Biblical Story

Jesus of Nazareth is the unmistakable centerpiece of the biblical story. The Gospels make it clear that his significance lies not simply in his death, but also especially in his person, life, and teaching. Nonetheless, each evangelist (Gospel writer) in his own way demonstrates by way of narrative that the death and resurrection of Jesus are the high points of his story (fully one-fourth to one-third of each Gospel is given over to the events of the final week).

Our interest in each of the Gospels is in their narrative about Jesus. Even though the first three are "synoptic" (seeing Jesus through common eyes), and Matthew and Luke use Mark in their telling of the story, they strike out on their own individual paths—all telling the same story, but each with his own concerns and emphases for the sake of his implied readers. Luke's Gospel is unique in yet another way, because he narrates the story of Jesus in two aspects: First, his Gospel, as do the others, tells about what Jesus "began to do and to teach" (Acts 1:1); second, in the book of Acts, he tells how the story of Jesus continues, now through the power of the Spirit, in the ministry of the early church.

The evangelists make it especially clear that you cannot understand Jesus without seeing how he fits into the Old Testament story that has preceded him—as the climax and fulfillment of the hopes expressed almost from the beginning of the story. On the one hand, they all see

Jesus as clearly fitting into the prophetic tradition—by his mighty words, mighty deeds, and symbolic actions (e.g., cleansing the temple; cursing the fig tree)—and so he is perceived by the crowds (Matt 21:46; Luke 7:16; 13:13). At the same time, all of them are writing from this side of the resurrection and know that he is none other than the expected "Son of David" (Mark 10:47–48), God's "Son" (Ps 2:7; Matt 3:17; 17:5; and parallels), who comes to his people as their King.

One key to this aspect of their narratives lies with the Old Testament understanding of the role of the king in Israel, who is often seen both to represent God to the people and to embody the people of Israel in his own person. This can be seen especially in the book of Psalms and in the suffering servant songs in Isaiah 42–53. It will be helpful for you as you read the Gospels to note how the evangelists tell the story of Jesus from this perspective. Take, for example, his baptism and the testing in the desert, where Jesus succeeds at the very places where Israel failed, as his own citations from Deuteronomy 6–8 make plain. Or take the discourse in John 15:1–8, where Jesus, picking up an image of Israel from the Old Testament (Ps 80:8–19; Isa 5:1–7; Jer 2:21), speaks of *himself* as the true vine and his disciples as the branches. And his death is clearly seen in light of Isaiah's suffering servant (Isa 52:13–53:12), as the one who bears the sins of the people, thus both representing the people and drawing them into the story themselves.

For each Gospel (and the book of Acts, too), therefore, we will also try to help you to see how the evangelist ties the story of Jesus to the story of Israel as the "fulfillment" of Jewish messianic hopes and expectations. Related to this, we also need to point out that each Gospel was written at a time when Gentile inclusion in the grand story (see comments on Gen 11:27–25:11, p. 30) was in full swing; we will therefore point out how each deals with this issue, especially in light of the rejection of Jesus by many of the Jews.

On other matters related to their composition and relationships to one another, as well as their essential message about the coming of the kingdom (as "already" and "not yet"), we point you to chapter 7 in *How to 1*.

The Gospel according to Matthew

ORIENTING DATA FOR MATTHEW

- **Content:** the story of Jesus, including large blocks of teaching, from the announcement of his birth to the commissioning of the disciples to make disciples of the Gentiles

- **Author:** anonymous; Papias (ca. A.D. 125) attributes "the first Gospel" to the apostle Matthew; scholarship is divided

- **Date:** unknown (since he used Mark, very likely written in the 70s or 80s)

- **Recipients:** unknown; but almost certainly Jewish Christians with a commitment to the Gentile mission, most commonly thought to have lived in and around Antioch of Syria

- **Emphases:** Jesus is the Son of God, the (messianic) King of the Jews; Jesus is God present with us in miraculous power; Jesus is the church's Lord; the teaching of Jesus has continuing importance for God's people; the gospel of the kingdom is for all peoples—Jew and Gentile alike

OVERVIEW OF MATTHEW

It is fitting that Matthew comes first in the New Testament, for two reasons: first, from the opening sentence it has deliberate and direct ties to the Old Testament; second, because of its orderly arrangement of Jesus' teaching, it was the most often used Gospel in the early church (cited by the early church fathers more than twice as often as the other Gospels).

The genius of Matthew's Gospel lies in its structure, which presents a marvelous tapestry of narrative interwoven with carefully crafted blocks of teaching. So well is this done that the most prominent feature of Matthew's story—the five blocks of teaching—is sometimes not even noticed because one is more aware of the flow of the narrative (which follows Mark very closely). The five blocks of teaching (5:1–7:29; 10:11–42; 13:1–52; 18:1–35; [23:1] 24:1–25:46) are presented on a topical basis. Each is marked off by a similar concluding formula ("When Jesus had finished [saying these things]"), which Matthew uses to transition back to the narrative.

The story itself begins with a twofold introduction about Jesus' origins (chs. 1–2) and about his preparations for public ministry (3:1–4:11). After that, each combined block of "narrative with discourse" forms a progressive aspect to the story, all having to do with Jesus, the messianic King, inaugurating the time of God's kingly rule—4:12–7:29, proclamation of and life in the kingdom; 8:1–10:42, the power and mission of the kingdom; 11:1–13:52, questioning and opposition to the kingdom and its mixed reception in the world; 13:53–18:35, growing opposition, confession by the disciples, and special instructions to the community of the King; 19:1–25:46, mixed responses to the Prophet who now presents himself as the King, and the judgment of those who reject him. The story concludes (chs. 26–28) with the trial, crucifixion, and resurrection of Jesus, and the commissioning of the disciples to take the story to the nations.

SPECIFIC ADVICE FOR READING MATTHEW

You cannot easily miss Matthew's way of tying the story of Jesus to that of Israel, since it is so direct and up-front. Jesus belongs to the genealogy of Israel's royal line, and he fulfills all kinds of prophetic messianic expectations. Note how often (eleven times in all) Matthew editorializes, "This was to fulfill what was said [spoken] through the prophet(s)." Moreover, Jesus' ministry and teaching presuppose the authoritative nature of the Old Testament law (5:17–48), and during his earthly ministry, Jesus focuses on the "lost sheep of Israel" (10:6).

But at the death of Jesus, the temple curtain is torn in two (27:51), indicating that its time is over and that the time of Jesus and his followers has begun. You will see as you go along how Matthew presents Jesus as being in unrelieved opposition to the Pharisees and the teachers of the law (e.g., 5:20; 12:38; 21:15; 22:15; 23:2–36), so much so that he speaks of "their [your] synagogue(s)" as over against his disciples (e.g., 10:17; 13:54; 23:34). And an alternative story explaining away Jesus' resurrection still circulated among some Jews at the time Matthew is writing (28:11–15).

At the same time, look for the ways that Matthew also exhibits clear concern for the mission to the Gentiles. For example, four women—primarily, if not all, Gentiles—are included in the genealogy (Tamar, Rahab, Ruth, and Uriah's wife [Bathsheba]). The story proper begins in Galilee (Matt 4:12–16), which Matthew sees as fulfilling Isaiah 9:1–2—that the people living in darkness, in Galilee of the Gentiles, have seen a great light—and it ends (Matt 28:16–20) with a commissioning of the apostles to make disciples of all the nations (= Gentiles).

This interweaving of themes suggests that the Gospel was written at a time when church and synagogue were now separated and were in conflict over who is in the true succession of the Old Testament promises. Matthew's way of answering this issue is by telling the story of Jesus, who "fulfills" every kind of Jewish messianic hope and expectation: After his birth as "king of the Jews" (2:2), he is honored (worshiped) by Eastern royal figures; at his birth, baptism, and transfiguration he is signaled as God's Son; his virgin birth fulfills Isaiah 7:14 that "God is with us" (cf. 12:6, 41, 42; 28:20); he dies as "THE KING OF THE JEWS," 27:37; and is acknowledged as "Son of God" by the Roman centurion (27:54). At the same time Matthew also recognizes Jesus as Isaiah's suffering servant (20:28) and extends this recognition to include his whole ministry, including his healings (8:17) and the opposition (12:17–21).

Equally important for Matthew, Jesus is presented as the true interpreter of the law (5:17–48; 7:24–27), especially over against the Pharisees and the teachers of the law. The latter have turned the law into a heavy yoke (11:28) and bind heavy burdens on people's backs (23:4); Jesus, who as Son knows and reveals the Father (11:25–27), offers an easy yoke and light burden (11:28–30). His "law" is mercy and grace (9:13; 12:7; 20:30, 34; 23:23). Those who experience such mercy are thus expected to be merciful in return (18:21–35; cf. 5:7). Jesus did not come to abolish the Law and Prophets but to fulfill them (5:17; 7:12), to bring the new righteousness of God's kingdom that goes infinitely beyond the teachings of the Pharisees (5:20). At the same time, Matthew shows concern about some within the believing community who prophesy but do not live obediently (7:15–23). In his Gospel, therefore, the twelve disciples play the role of learners who are to model life in the kingdom. You will want to look for these features as you read.

Thus, for Matthew, Jesus is the center of everything, and those who follow him not only proclaim the coming of the kingdom—the coming of God's mercy to sinners—but they are also expected to live like him (7:15–23). And when they have success in their own proclamation of the kingdom, especially among Gentiles, they are to make disciples of them by teaching them to observe the way of Jesus (28:19–20), both in their individual lives (chs. 5–7) and in their church communities (ch. 18). Matthew almost certainly intends his Gospel to serve as the manual for such instruction!

A WALK THROUGH MATTHEW

☐ **1:1–2:23** *Prologue: Jesus' Divine and Human Origins*

Here you find the well-known features of Matthew's narrative of Jesus' origins (the annunciation to Joseph; the visit of the Magi; the slaughter of the innocents; the flight to Egypt). As you read, note how many of Matthew's concerns and themes surface here. His genealogy explicitly places Jesus in the royal lineage (son of David) and anticipates the Gentile mission (son of Abraham). His birth from a virgin both fulfills prophecy and emphasizes his divine origins (by the Holy Spirit, as "God with us"). Note especially how the narrative of chapter 2 places worship of Jesus by Gentile royal court figures in the context of an attempted execution by Jewish royalty.

☐ **3:1–4:11** *Introduction to Jesus: His Baptism and the Testing*

Jesus is introduced to Israel by way of a new prophet, John the Baptist; John consents to baptize him (how could the Messiah accept a baptism for repentance?). Jesus is immediately led by the Spirit into the desert to be tested as to who he is (Son of God) and why he is here (his royal/suffering servant mission). Note how in his baptism and forty-day testing Jesus steps into the role of Israel (= through the Red Sea followed by forty years in the desert) and foils Satan with passages from Deuteronomy 6 and 8, precisely at points where Israel failed the test; thus the (now humble) Divine Warrior wins the first round against the enemy.

☐ **4:12–7:29** *The Proclamation of the Kingdom*

The *narrative* portion of part 1 is very brief: Starting in Galilee of the Gentiles, Jesus gathers disciples, proclaims the good news of the kingdom, and heals the sick (note the summary nature of 4:23–25; the first actual "miracle stories" appear in the next section).

The *discourse* in this case is by far the best known. Set in the context of a mountain (as Moses on Sinai), the new Torah (teaching from the law) is the carefully structured Sermon on the Mount, much of which you will recognize even if you have never read Matthew before. The collection emphasizes first the "gospel" setting of the discourse (5:3–16, nine beatitudes, plus affirmations of God's people being salt and light).

The rest instructs the disciples on the new righteousness (the way of living in the kingdom), setting it in the context of "fulfilling" the Law and Prophets (5:17) and going beyond that of the Pharisees and the teachers of the law (traditionally "scribes") in every way—especially ethical life over against the scribes (5:21–48) and the three religious duties of the Pharisees, namely, almsgiving, prayer, and fasting (6:1–18).

These are followed by admonitions to single-hearted trust in God, which renders life in the kingdom as without anxiety (6:19–34), to just treatment of others (7:1–12), and to obedience (7:13–27). Note the conclusion in 7:28–29, "When Jesus had finished saying these things."

☐ 8:1–10:42   *The Power and Mission of the Kingdom*

The *narrative* portion of part 2 is dominated by eight miracle stories (that contain nine actual miracles). Notice how these stories emphasize the power of the kingdom, beginning with mercy for an outcast (8:1–4) and a Gentile (8:5–13), and they include triumph over the raging sea and over demons. And so the humble Divine Warrior wins round two against Satan. Included also are three short narratives that in turn illustrate the cost of discipleship (8:18–22) and the beginning of opposition (9:9–17); note especially the citation from Hosea 6:6, "I desire mercy, not sacrifice" (Matt 9:13), in the context of opposition. A nearly identical summary (9:35–38) to what you read in 4:23–25 sets the stage for the second discourse.

The *discourse* in this section is set in the context of Jesus' sending out of the Twelve (10:1–14)—the workers sent out "into his harvest field" (9:37–38). But as the collection of sayings proceeds (beginning with 10:17), you will see that they speak primarily to the church's later mission in the world, especially anticipating the rough reception those who carry on the mission of Jesus are going to experience in days to come. Note how the summarizing statement begins the next section (11:1a).

☐ **11:1 – 13:52** *Questioning of and Opposition to Jesus and the Kingdom*

In the *narrative* part of this section, be looking for the rough reception that Jesus himself experienced as he is both questioned and opposed by "this generation" (11:1 – 19; 12:1 – 14). Note how these two narratives bracket Jesus' judgment on unrepentant Israel (11:20 – 24) and his invitation to the humble, the "little children" who are oppressed by the burden of Pharisaism (11:25 – 30). And note how Matthew includes a second time the citation of Hosea 6:6, "I desire mercy, not sacrifice" (Matt 12:7), again in the context of opposition.

The opposition is seen as "fulfillment" regarding Jesus as Isaiah's suffering servant (12:15 – 21; citing Isa 42:1 – 4, the first of the servant songs). This is followed by two more narratives of opposition (Matt 12:22 – 45, God's stronger man has come and bound the strong man and is plundering his house [the Divine Warrior theme again], and one affirming the humble poor who follow Jesus and do God's will [12:46 – 50]).

You will recognize the *discourse* to be made up of seven parables (13:1 – 52). Note their generally common thread — instructing the disciples on the mixed reception of the kingdom in the world, which will be made evident at the end, while two of them (13:44 – 46) emphasize the surpassing worth of the kingdom. Again, watch how the opening sentence of the next section serves to summarize this discourse.

☐ **13:53 – 18:35** *Opposition to and Confession of Jesus*

As you read the *narrative* portion of part 4 (13:53 – 17:27), watch for the ways it further illustrates preceding themes (varied responses to Jesus from ch. 13) while at the same time gains momentum toward the final week in Jerusalem.

It begins with the rejection of God's prophets (Jesus in his hometown, 13:53 – 58; John the Baptist by Herod, 14:1 – 12), followed by two mighty deeds (14:13 – 36). Matthew then sets controversy with the Pharisees (15:1 – 20) in contrast with the faith of a Gentile woman (15:21 – 28).

Note how a second feeding miracle (15:29 – 39) leads to Jesus' being tested by the Pharisees and Saduccees (16:1 – 4), which in turn leads Jesus to warn his disciples against their teaching (vv. 5 – 12), all of which leads to the climactic moment in verses 13 – 20, when the disciples confess Jesus as the Messiah. This leads in turn to their being let in on what is to come — Jesus' death in Jerusalem (vv. 21 – 23) — which in turn leads to special instruction on discipleship (vv. 24–28), while three of them see his resurrection glory in advance (17:1–13).

Another triumph over demons provides for teaching on faith (17:14–21), followed by a second prediction of Jesus' death (vv. 22–23) and his announcement that his followers are exempt from temple regulations (vv. 24–27).

Note how the *discourse* in this section (ch. 18) picks up the discipleship theme from the preceding narrative, being singularly concerned with relationships within the believing community. After establishing the nature of discipleship (God's "little ones," the humble poor), Matthew includes instructions—not causing the little ones to stumble (vv. 6–9), seeking the wandering ones (vv. 10–14), dealing with sin against one another (vv. 15–20), and forgiveness (vv. 21–35). Again note how the first sentence in the next section concludes this discourse.

☐ **19:1–25:46** *Jerusalem Receives and Rejects Her King*

Be watching here as the *narrative* portion of this final section (19:1–22:46) puts Jesus first in "the region of Judea" (19:1) and then in Jerusalem itself (21:1), which Jesus enters for the events of the final week. You will observe that the narratives in the first half (chs. 19–20) continue the themes of opposition and discipleship. After opposing the Pharisees' easy view of divorce (19:1–12), the childlike nature of discipleship is reinforced over against the rich, who find it difficult to enter the kingdom (vv. 13–15, 16–26).

This leads to further instruction on discipleship—the "last" will be "first" in the kingdom (19:27–30); they are the undeserving who receive mercy, to the consternation of those who consider themselves worthy (20:1–16). Yet the disciples are still not fully on board, as a third passion prediction (vv. 17–19) is followed by a desire for positions of authority in the kingdom (vv. 20–24). Jesus responds by assuming the role of the suffering servant (vv. 25–28), which they are to model.

On the way to Jerusalem Jesus heals two blind men (20:29–34; the eyes of the blind are opened, while those who see will be shown to be blind). Then Jesus presents himself to Israel as its long-awaited King (21:1–11, fulfilling Zech 9:9 and Ps 118:25–26) and marks off the temple as his own (Matt 21:12–17; cf. Mal 3:1–4). You will see that most of the rest of this narrative (Matt 21:23–22:46) is a series of "conflict stories" interspersed with parables, which together illustrate the clash over

Jesus' authority that will lead to his execution. Note especially the role that Psalms 118 and 110 play in these events.

The *discourse* that follows is prophetic, first announcing judgment on the teachers of the law and the Pharisees (23:1–39), after which Jesus leaves the temple ("your house is left to you desolate," 23:38) and pronounces judgment against Jerusalem (24:1–28) in light of the end itself (vv. 29–35), calling for watchfulness and service on the part of his followers (24:36–25:46).

☐ 26:1–28:20   *The King Is Tried, Crucified, and Raised*

Here you come to the climax of the Gospel—the final rejection of Jesus in Jerusalem (26:1–27:66), including the trial, denial, crucifixion, death, and burial of Jesus. Note Matthew's interest in two events at Jesus' death that mark the end of the old and the beginning of the new: (1) The temple curtain was torn in two, and (2) some holy people from the former era were raised to life (27:51–53).

But the conclusion offers hope for the future: "He is not here; he has risen, just as he said" (28:1–10). After noting an alternative report that was circulating among the Jews who opposed Matthew's church (vv. 11–15), he concludes with the commissioning of the disciples and the affirmation that all authority belongs to the risen Lord, who is still present with us to the end of the age as we continue to carry out their commission from him (vv. 16–20).

What a wonderful way to begin the New Testament part of God's story—of his saving a people for his Name through the death and resurrection of Jesus, and sending them into the world to be the bearers of his Good News and to make disciples from all the nations, thus fulfilling the Abrahamic covenant!

The Gospel according to Mark

ORIENTING DATA FOR MARK

- **Content:** the story of Jesus from his baptism to his resurrection, about two-thirds of which tells of his ministry in Galilee, while the last third narrates his final week in Jerusalem

- **Author:** anonymous; attributed (by Papias, ca. A.D. 125) to John Mark, a sometime companion of Paul (Col 4:10) and later of Peter (1 Pet 5:13)

- **Date:** ca. A.D. 65 (according to Papias, soon after the deaths of Paul and Peter in Rome)

- **Recipients:** the church in Rome (according to Papias), which accounts for its preservation along with the longer Matthew and Luke

- **Emphases:** the time of God's rule (the kingdom of God) has come with Jesus; Jesus has brought about the new exodus promised in Isaiah; the kingly Messiah came in weakness, his identity a secret except to those to whom it is revealed; the way of the new exodus leads to Jesus' death in Jerusalem; the way of discipleship is to take up a cross and follow him

OVERVIEW OF MARK

Although Mark is the earliest of the four Gospels (see *How to 1*, pp. 135–39), because it is shorter and has much less teaching than the others, it has often tended to suffer neglect. At one level his story is straightforward. After a prologue, which introduces us to the good news about Jesus Christ (1:1–15), the story unfolds in four parts. In part 1 (1:16–3:6), Jesus goes public with the announcement of the kingdom. With rapid-fire action he calls disciples, drives out demons, heals the sick, and announces that all of this has to do with the coming of God's rule; in the process he draws amazement from the crowds and opposition from the religious and political establishment, who early on plot his death.

Part 2 (3:7 – 8:21) develops the role of the three significant groups. Jesus' miracles and teaching are sources of constant amazement to the *crowds;* the *disciples* receive private instruction (4:13, 34) and join in the proclamation (6:7 – 13), but are slow to understand (8:14 – 21; cf. 6:52); the *opposition* continues to mount (7:1 – 23; 8:11 – 13).

In part 3 (8:22 – 10:45), Jesus directs his attention primarily to the disciples. Three times he explains the nature of his kingship—and hence of discipleship (8:34 – 38)—as going the way of the cross (as Isaiah's suffering servant; Mark 10:45), and three times the disciples completely miss it.

Part 4 (10:46 – 15:47) brings the story to its climax. The king enters Jerusalem and the crowds go wild with excitement, but in the end the opposition has its day. Jesus is put on trial, found guilty, and turned over to the Romans for execution on a cross—as "the king of the Jews" (15:2).

A brief epilogue (16:1 – 8) reminds Mark's readers that "[Jesus] has risen!"

SPECIFIC ADVICE FOR READING MARK

It was a killing time in Rome. The church was experiencing the Neronian holocaust, in which many believers had been burned alive at Nero's garden parties and two of the church's more important figures (Peter and Paul) had been executed. Soon after, there appeared among them a small book (Mark's Gospel), written to remind them of the nature of Jesus' own messiahship (as God's suffering servant) and to encourage cross-bearing discipleship.

Mark has been described as one who cannot tell a story badly. In part this is due to his vivid style, which is what also gives his Gospel the sense of being rapid-fire. Almost every sentence begins with "and" (cf. KJV); forty-one times he begins with "and immediately" (which does not always refer to time but to the urgency of the telling), and twenty-five times with "and again." But he also includes little details, including the Aramaic words of Jesus on six occasions. All of this reflects both a written form of oral recounting and the memory of an eyewitness.

The prominent place of Peter in the Gospel and the fact that early on so much happens in and around Peter's house in Capernaum suggest that the tradition has it right—that the Gospel in part reflects Peter's own telling of the story. But Peter's role in the Gospel is anything but that of a hero. He who urged others to "clothe yourselves in humility" (1 Pet 5:5) does not forget his own weaknesses while following Jesus; you will want to look for these features as you read. But at the end, after he vehemently denied knowing his Lord (Mark 14:66–72), he also remembers that the angel told the women at the tomb, "Go, tell his disciples *and Peter*" (16:7, emphasis added).

But brief and breathtaking as Mark's Gospel is, it is not at all simple. Indeed, Mark tells the story with profound theological insight. Absolutely crucial to your reading with understanding is to note how he presents Jesus as Messiah. Three things emerge at the beginning that carry all the way through to the end: (1) Jesus is the kingly Messiah, (2) Jesus is God's suffering servant, and (3) Jesus keeps his identity secret.

Mark's telling of the story thus emphasizes the "messianic secret," the "mystery of the kingdom of God," namely, that the expected coming King knew he was destined to suffer for the sake of the people. The demons, who recognize him, are silenced (1:25, 34; 3:11–12); the crowds to whom the King comes with compassion are told not to tell anyone about his miracles (1:44; 5:43; 7:36; 8:26); when finally confessed as Messiah by the disciples, he tells them to tell no one (8:30). What no one expects is for God's King to be impaled on a cross! But Jesus knows—and he silences all messianic fervor, lest it thwart the divine plan that leads to the cross. When the disciples are clued in to the "mystery," even they fail to get it (8:27–33); they are like the blind man who has to be touched twice (8:22–26; in their case, by Jesus' resurrection).

But in reminding his readers of the nature of Jesus' messiahship, Mark also reminds us that this is the way of discipleship as well. Indeed, the first instruction on discipleship (8:34), which calls for cross bearing, appears only after the first disclosure to the disciples of Jesus' own impending death (v. 31).

Mark also uses the theme of God's kingly suffering Messiah to show Jesus' connection to the story of Israel, especially Isaiah's (now long-delayed) new exodus. The key moments in the first exodus are deliverance, the journey through the desert, and arrival at the place where the Lord dwells. Isaiah (chs. 35; 40–55) announces the return from Babylonian exile as a new exodus.

Notice how Mark puts us in touch with this theme in his very first sentence: "The beginning of the gospel about Jesus the Messiah, as it is written in Isaiah the prophet." Jesus then steps into the role of Israel (through the water and testing in the desert). The theme carries all the way through. Mark *cites* Isaiah at key points (the opposition's hardness of heart, "those on the outside" [Mark 4:10–12; 7:6; 9:48]; the inclusion of Gentiles [11:17]). He echoes Isaiah in all kinds of ways: Jesus' ministry is expressed in the language of Isaiah 53 (Mark 10:45); the parable of the tenants (12:1–12) recasts Isaiah's "song of the vineyard" (Isa 5:1–7); the motif of eyes that see but don't perceive and ears that hear but don't understand (Isa 6:9–10). The long-awaited Deliverer has now come, but contrary to common expectations, he has come to suffer for the people in order to lead them from exile into the final promised land (Mark 13).

A significant part of the new exodus included the gathering of the Gentile nations. Since Mark's Gospel is intended for people who are already a part of that mission, his way of placing them in the story of Jesus is by relating a series of non-Galilean (Gentile) narratives in 6:53–9:29. In this context he places the matter of ceremonial washing, for example, and he comments that Jesus in effect abolished the food laws (7:19b). Moreover, the Gentile mission delays the dropping of the final curtain on history (13:10), and in repossessing the temple as Israel's "king" (11:17), Jesus cites Isaiah 56:7 ("my house will be called a house of prayer for all nations" [= Gentiles]).

By looking for these various features as you read, you may find yourself among those who know Mark's Gospel as one of the rich treasures in the Bible.

A WALK THROUGH MARK

The Prologue—Introduction to Jesus and the Kingdom (1:1–15)

As you read Mark's very brief introduction, notice how all of his major concerns appear here. The "good news about Jesus" begins with the announcement that Isaiah's new exodus has begun: "Prepare the way for the Lord" (1:3), proclaims John the Baptist—the new Elijah (Mal 4:5–6)—who thus presents Jesus to Israel. Jesus then assumes the role of Israel in the new exodus. At his baptism the voice from heaven defines Jesus' messianic destiny in words from Psalm 2:7 (the Davidic king), Genesis 22:2 (God's beloved Son), and Isaiah 42:1 (God's suffering servant). After his testing in the desert, he comes into Galilee announcing the "good news of God": "the time has come" for God's kingdom to appear, which calls for faith and repentance.

Part 1: The Kingdom Goes Public — Disciples, Crowds, Opposition (1:16–3:6)

☐ **1:16–45 The Disciples and the Crowds**

Note how Mark starts the story with the call of disciples to "come, follow [Jesus]" (1:16–20), a key to much of the Gospel. Even so, the disciples are in the background for most of this section, as Mark focuses first on the crowds (vv. 21–45). They are the "amazed" on whom Jesus has compassion and with whom he has immense popularity (vv. 22, 27–28, 32–33, 37–38, 45)—so much so that at the end of the short narrative, Jesus can "no longer enter a town openly." Note that Mark accomplishes all this with just three short narratives!

☐ **2:1–3:6 The Opposition**

Now comes the opposition (2:1–3:6), presented in a series of five narratives. Look for the question "why?" in each of the first four, whereby Mark shows the *reasons* for opposition: 2:7 (blasphemy = making himself equal with God); 2:16 (eating with sinners); 2:18 (failure to keep the rules); 2:24 (breaking the Sabbath). Note at the end (3:6) the solidifying of the opposition—both religious and political—with the first hint of Jesus' coming death.

Part 2: The Mystery of the Kingdom — Faith, Misunderstanding, Hard Hearts (3:7–8:21)

☐ **3:7–4:34 Presenting the Mystery of the Kingdom**

The plot thickens. Notice how the three groups are immediately brought back into the picture (crowds, 3:7–12; disciples, vv. 13–19; opposition, vv. 20–30; even his family is bewildered, vv. 31–34). The disciples are now "appointed" as the Twelve (representing the remnant of Israel), and their role is stepped up considerably.

In 4:1–34 Mark uses Jesus' teaching in parables to introduce the mystery of the kingdom, which will be revealed to them (those on the inside). The opposition (those "on the outside"), in their failure to hear with their ears (4:9), fulfill Isaiah's prophecy (Isa 6:9–10; cf. his scathing rebuke of people becoming like their idols that cannot hear [Isa 42:18, 20]), but as the story proceeds, the disciples fare little better.

☐ **4:35 – 6:6a   The Kingdom Present in Power: The Blindness of the World**

Next you encounter a series of mighty deeds (4:35 – 5:43). In turn Jesus displays his power over the sea, demons, death, and uncleanness (an "untouchable" [cf. Lev 15:25 – 27] touches Jesus and is made whole, thus restored to life in the community). Note the emphasis on *faith:* those to whom the mystery is being revealed lack faith (Mark 4:40); the people across the lake want Jesus to leave (5:17); the woman's faith makes her whole (5:34); the synagogue leader is encouraged to have faith (5:36); Jesus' hometown lacks faith (6:6a). Wonder and awe come easy; true faith does not.

☐ **6:6b – 8:21   The Kingdom Extends to Gentiles: The Blindness of the Disciples**

Watch for two things in this section: (1) the role of the disciples and (2) Jesus' ministry among Gentiles. It begins with the Twelve joining Jesus in ministry—with such success that Herod gets wind of it (6:6b – 30). But note how the two "feeding" stories (6:31 – 44; 8:1 – 10) are both followed by the "hardness of heart" motif (6:45 – 52; 8:11 – 21).

In between (6:53 – 7:37), Jesus ministers among the Gentiles, who show both faith (7:24 – 30) and amazement (vv. 31 – 37). Significantly, Mark brings the Pharisees into this scene as well, as Jesus eliminates the food laws by pronouncing all things clean (7:1 – 23).

The "hardness of heart" narrative at the end (8:11 – 21) is especially important to Mark's narrative. The Pharisees "test" Jesus about "a sign from heaven"; they are looking for a Messiah of worldly power. When his disciples fail to understand his warning about the Pharisees, note how his questions reflect Isaiah 6:9 – 10 (cf. Mark 4:9 – 12): "Do you have eyes but fail to see, and ears but fail to hear?" (8:18).

Part 3: The Mystery Unveiled—The Cross and the Way of Discipleship (8:22 – 10:45)

You can scarcely miss the central feature of this section, which frames the whole, namely, the three passion predictions and the disciples' hardness of heart. Thus the crowds and opposition recede into the background, while Jesus, on the way to Jerusalem, devotes himself primarily to instructing the disciples.

☐ 8:22–9:29   *The First Passion Prediction and Its Aftermath*

Note how the narrative of the twice-touched blind man (8:22–26) serves to bridge the disciples' "blindness" (vv. 17–21) and their "first touch" at Caesarea Philippi (vv. 27–30). But they clearly need a second touch. Peter gives the right answer: Jesus is the Messiah. But when told that the Messiah must die, he is infused with "the yeast of the Pharisees" and vehemently rejects such a wild idea (vv. 31–33).

Watch for two things in the crucial teaching on discipleship that follows (8:34–9:1): (1) This is the first instruction on discipleship in the Gospel (coming only after the nature of Jesus' messiahship is disclosed), and (2) here the crowds are (significantly) included.

The Transfiguration (9:2–13), with its affirmation of the Son as the one to hear, is the divine response to Jesus' suffering before it happens; note how both the Law (Moses) and the Prophets (Elijah) are witnesses. But it is also set in contrast to the continuing hardness of heart on the part of the disciples (Peter on the mountain, and the rest with the demon-possessed boy, 9:14–29).

☐ 9:30–10:31   *The Second Passion Prediction and Its Aftermath*

Watch how the second foretelling of Jesus' death is now followed by squabbling among the disciples over who is the greatest (9:33–34). Jesus responds by pointing out the nature of discipleship—servanthood and childlikeness (vv. 35–37). Note how this theme is immediately picked up in the instructions that follow—on welcoming Jesus' little ones and not causing them to sin (vv. 38–50). When Mark returns to it in 10:13–16, he sets it in contrast to the rich (10:17–31), for whom it is hard "to enter the kingdom of God"—an obvious shock to the disciples, who assume the rich have God's blessing.

☐ 10:32–45   *The Third Passion Prediction and Its Aftermath*

One more time, but briefly in this case, Mark points to the disciples' hardness of heart. Note that this time it is set in the context of "on their way up to Jerusalem." So while Jesus is heading toward his death as God's suffering servant (v. 45), the disciples covet positions of authority!

Part 4: The King Comes to Jerusalem to Die (10:46–15:47)

In this section you will see the religious opposition coming to the fore, while the disciples and crowds play only supportive roles.

☐ 10:46–13:27   *The King Comes to Jerusalem: The House Is Divided*

Note how the Bartimaeus story (10:46–52) serves as the bridge to this section—a blind man, who "sees" Jesus as "the Son of David," is given sight, while the seeing, who don't recognize David's son (12:35–40), remain blind. You might want to check out how this narrative and the next two (triumphal entry and cleansing/judgment of the temple) echo God's coming to Israel in Isaiah 35.

Thus with three prophetic symbolic actions—the triumphal entry, the cursing of the fig tree, and the cleansing of the temple—Jesus presents himself to Israel as their long-awaited King. The Lord whom they seek comes suddenly to his temple—but in judgment (see Mal 3:1). This is followed by a series of six conflict stories between Jesus and the religious authorities (Mark 11:27–12:40), to which the widow with her two small coins stands in bold relief (12:41–44).

The disciples reappear in chapter 13 to hear the announcement of God's eventual judgment on Jerusalem (vv. 14–23) in the context of final judgment and salvation (vv. 24–27), with emphasis on the disciples' being watchful.

☐ 14:1–15:47   *The King Is Crucified*

Finally the story reaches its dreadful/marvelous climax. The King is anointed for burial (14:1–11) and has a final meal with his disciples, who are assured they will eat and drink anew with him in the coming kingdom (vv. 12–26)—and this in the context of their present disowning of him (vv. 27–31, 66–72). He is then led away to be humiliated by the religious opposition, as they spit on the Messiah (vv. 32–65) before turning him over to Rome to be executed by crucifixion (15:1–41), as "the king of the Jews." What Pilate intended as warning—this is what happens to messianic pretenders—Mark sees as the ultimate truth about Jesus as kingly Messiah. Jesus is then buried under the watchful eye of some women who will be the first to hear the good news of his resurrection.

Epilogue: The Story Is Not Over (16:1–8)

The epilogue remains a mystery. Jesus has been raised (but no recorded appearances); the story obviously goes on, but the final word is fear. Did Mark write more that was lost (see the two later endings in the New Revised Standard Version)? Or did he intend his readers to change "fear" into "awe," and follow Jesus along the way that leads to the cross and the resurrection? We may never know, but the latter is certainly what he intends his Gospel as a whole to do.

This superb telling of the story of Jesus as the fulfillment of the story of Israel is crucial to our understanding the emphases of much of the rest of the New Testament, especially the letters of Paul and the books of Hebrews and 1 Peter. As Paul put it in 1 Corinthians 1:18–25, in the weakness and folly of a crucified Messiah, God has shown his power and wisdom at work in the world for salvation.

The Gospel according to Luke

ORIENTING DATA FOR LUKE

- **Content:** the story of Jesus as part 1 of Luke-Acts, which is the story of the salvation of "Israel," which Christ and the Spirit have brought about; part 1 begins with the announcement of Jesus' birth by the Spirit and carries through to his ascension

- **Author:** according to very early tradition, Luke the physician and sometime companion of the apostle Paul (see Col 4:14), the only Gentile author in the Bible

- **Date:** uncertain; scholars are divided between a date before the death of Paul (ca. A.D. 64; see Acts 28:30–31) and one after the fall of Jerusalem (A.D. 70, because of his use of Mark)

- **Recipient(s):** Theophilus is otherwise unknown; in keeping with such prefaces in Greco-Roman literature, he was probably the patron of Luke-Acts, thus underwriting its publication; the implied readers are Gentile Christians, whose place in God's story is ensured through the work of Jesus Christ and the Spirit

- **Emphases:** God's Messiah has come to his people, Israel, with the promised inclusion of Gentiles; Jesus came to save the lost, including every kind of marginalized person whom traditional religion would put outside the boundaries; Jesus' ministry is carried out under the power of the Holy Spirit; the necessity of Jesus' death and resurrection (which fulfilled Old Testament promises) for the forgiveness of sins

OVERVIEW OF LUKE

If Mark is one of those who cannot tell a story badly, Luke is the one who can tell it to perfection. His vision is all-embracing: The story of Jesus, now placed in the context of world history (Luke 2:1; 3:1–2), includes the Spirit's ongoing ministry in the church as well. So you need to read part 1 in connection with part 2, as Luke himself intended, and not just in the context of the other three Gospels (thus we will guide you through Acts in the next chapter, out of canonical order). Luke's story is thus in two major parts: (1) how the good news of God's salvation for all people began, through the power of the Spirit, with Jesus in Galilee and in Jerusalem (Luke's Gospel), and (2) how the good news of God's salvation through Jesus was, by the power of the Spirit, carried by the apostles from Jerusalem to Rome (Acts).

Chapters 1 and 2 of Luke both introduce the story and anticipate all its major themes and concerns—the links with Old Testament promises; the Davidic kingly role of Jesus; the restoration of Israel; the inclusion of Gentiles; God's concern for the poor; the role of the Holy Spirit; the anticipated opposition; the joy caused by the good news about Jesus.

In 3:1–4:13 the ministries of John and Jesus are linked, as anticipated in chapter 1. Jesus is presented to Israel through his baptism and testing; he is also linked to the Gentile mission by a genealogy that takes him back through Abraham to Adam.

The rest of the Gospel is in three parts, set off by geographical notations. In 4:14–9:50 Jesus teaches and heals in Galilee. The introductory narrative of a Sabbath in Nazareth (4:16–30) serves as a prototype for the rest of the story—fulfillment of Old Testament promises; the Spirit descending on the Messiah; good news to the poor; inclusion of Gentiles; rejection by some of Israel.

In 9:51 Jesus "resolutely set out for Jerusalem"; he does not arrive there until 19:45. Although regularly portrayed in this long section as on the way to Jerusalem (10:38; 13:22; 17:11; 18:31), Jesus still gathers disciples around him, challenges all with his teachings, rejects a pharisaic understanding of God, and in turn is finally rejected by the religious and political authorities.

Finally in Jerusalem (19:45–24:53), Jesus is rejected by the Jewish leaders and is crucified. But the crucifixion and resurrection were of divine necessity—evidence of God's faithfulness to his people. So part

1 ends with the ascension and on a note of joy, as the disciples stay at the temple, awaiting part 2.

SPECIFIC ADVICE FOR READING LUKE

Luke's primary concern (in both parts) is with the story of salvation—God's salvation of "Israel," with its promised inclusion of the Gentiles. Salvation for Luke means God's acceptance and forgiveness of sinners, which, picking up an Old Testament theme, is especially expressed as "good news to the poor" (4:18; 7:22; cf. 1:51–53)—all those who have been marginalized by society at large and especially by the religious power brokers. They are the "lost" (19:10) and include wealthy tax collectors (19:1–9), "the [economically] poor, the crippled, the lame, the blind" (14:13; cf. 16:19–31), a Samaritan (17:11–19; cf. 10:25–37), and women (7:36–50; 8:2–3; 10:38–42; cf. the three women in chs. 1–2). Be looking for these as you read. It also includes the Gentiles, but that dimension of the story is reserved for Acts. Thus in part 1 the universalizing of salvation is vertical, covering every strata of society within Israel; in part 2 it is horizontal, focusing especially on the Gentiles and the march of the gospel from Jerusalem to Rome.

Thus in Luke's Gospel Jesus comes both as Israel's kingly Messiah (the announcement to Mary [1:32–33] is full of the language of the Davidic covenant from 2 Sam 7:14, 16) and as the one who has come to help God's "servant Israel, remembering to be merciful to Abraham and his descendants forever, just as he promised our ancestors" (Luke 1:54–55; cf. 1:68–75; 2:30–32). Luke begins part 2 with the disciples' question, "Lord, are you at this time going to restore the kingdom to Israel?" (Acts 1:6).

It is in this context that the temple (Zion) plays a significant role in Luke-Acts. Not only is the Messiah presented—and recognized—in the temple (Luke 2:21–38), but the only narrative of Jesus' childhood in the Gospels (2:41–52) places him in the temple courts having discussions with the teachers. This anticipates his return to the temple to teach in 20:1–21:38, after he had "cleansed" it (19:45–48). Fittingly, the outpouring of the Holy Spirit and the first proclaiming of the gospel happen at the temple in Acts 2–6. But the God who has thus returned to his earthly temple has also announced its coming destruction (Luke 21:20–24); in this new era of salvation God no longer dwells in a temple made by hands (Acts 7:48–50). And that leads to the other side of the story—that many in Israel, especially the "religious" and their leaders, reject Jesus, thus fulfilling Simeon's prophecy (Luke 2:34)—"This child is destined to cause the falling and rising of many in Israel, and to be a sign that will be spoken against." This begins in the programmatic narrative in 4:16–30 and continues throughout the Gospel, climaxing at the end with the rejection of Jesus by the Jewish leaders in Jerusalem. It becomes a major theme in Acts.

In this regard, watch especially for the significant role the books of Isaiah and the Psalms play in Luke's presentation. Isaiah's concern for the nations in the context of Jewish rejection frames the whole of Luke-Acts, beginning with Simeon's echo of Isaiah 49:6 (Luke 2:32), followed by Luke's own citation of Isaiah 40:3–5 regarding John the Baptist (Luke 3:4–6, "and all people will see God's salvation"), and finally with Jesus' citation of Isaiah 61:1–2 as he begins his public ministry (Luke 4:18–19). At the very end (Acts 28:26–27), Diaspora Jewish rejection of Jesus in Rome is seen to fulfill Isaiah 6:9–10 (cf. the citation of Isa 49:6 in the significant speech by Paul in Acts 13:47). At the same time Isaiah's suffering servant is the key to understanding Jesus' earthly ministry (Luke 22:37; Acts 8:32–33; cf. Mark), while Jesus' coming to the temple as Israel's rightful King and his present exaltation as Lord are seen in light of Psalms 2, 118, and 110 (see Luke 20:17, 42–43; Acts 2:34–35; 4:11, 25–26; cf. 7:56; cf. Hebrews).

Although salvation comes through Jesus, Luke especially emphasizes the role the Holy Spirit plays in God's salvation. You will notice how the Spirit predominates in the events in chapters 1–2 of Luke's Gospel, as well as in the ministry of Jesus himself. Everything Jesus does by way of preparation (3:1–4:11) is guided by the Spirit. His ministry begins with the citation of Isaiah 61:1, "the Spirit of the Lord is on me because he has anointed me" (4:18). That Luke intends his readers mentally to insert "by the Spirit" throughout this narrative about his earthly ministry is made clear by Peter in Acts 10:38—"how God anointed Jesus of Nazareth with the Holy Spirit and power, and how he went around doing good and healing all who were under the power of the devil, because God was with him." This theme is thoroughgoing in Acts.

You should also note the emphasis throughout the Gospel on prayer and joy. Jesus himself prays at every major point in the story, and Luke includes more *teaching* on prayer than all the other Gospels. And salvation as "good news for the poor" causes people regularly to glorify God with great joy. Here is one Gentile who is deeply grateful to be included in God's salvation of his people Israel.

A WALK THROUGH LUKE

The Story Begins (1:1–4:13)

☐ 1:1–4   The Prologue

Luke's preface follows a well-known literary convention, where an author sets forth the *reason* for his narrative, usually in light of what others have done and almost always addressing his patron as someone to be honored. Luke himself learned of the events about Jesus from some who were eyewitnesses (including Mary? see 2:51); he also knew of earlier such narratives (Mark was one of these, which he used in writing his own account).

☐ 1:5–2:52   The Announcement and Birth of Jesus, the Messiah

Four things are important to watch for here: (1) Luke deliberately ties the story of Jesus to Israel; for example, the story of Elizabeth and John echoes that of Hannah (1 Sam 1–2), the mother of Samuel—the prophet who anointed David; the Messiah's birth is announced to Mary in the language of the Davidic covenant (2 Sam 7:14, 16); Mary bursts into a song that echoes the Psalter, as does John's father, Zechariah, at John's birth. God is at last "remembering to be merciful to Abraham and his descendants" (Luke 1:54–55), to raise up "a horn of salvation for us in the house of David" (1:69). The narrative concludes (2:52) in words that echo the growth of young Samuel (1 Sam 2:26).

(2) All the people involved are among the poor of Israel. Thus (in chapter 2), Jesus is born in a manger because there was no guest room; his birth is announced to lowly shepherds; at Jesus' and Mary's "purification," his parents offer the sacrifice of the poorest of the poor; a widow prophesies about Jesus. (3) Simeon's blessing and prophecy are especially programmatic: Jesus will be the glory of Israel, he will bring salvation to the nations, and he will "cause the falling and rising of many in Israel." (4) Luke especially emphasizes Jesus' humanity (see 2:52); the miraculous element is regularly attributed to the work of the Spirit. The whole story develops in this mode.

☐ 3:1–4:13   Jesus' Preparation for Ministry

Already linked to Jesus in chapter 1, John the Baptist comes on the scene announcing the new exodus. But John is not the Messiah; rather, he points people to the coming of the Messiah (and his baptism with the Holy Spirit and fire). Jesus is baptized and is himself anointed by the Spirit. After a genealogy (tracing Jesus back to Adam), the Spirit leads him into the desert to be tested (as was Israel following its "baptism" through the Red Sea). And so Jesus is prepared for his public ministry.

The Ministry of Jesus in Galilee (4:14–9:50)

In this first major section of his Gospel, Luke weaves together a series of short narratives that illustrate Jesus' powerful ministry on behalf of the poor and the captives; also included are several illustrations of his teachings, with emphasis on hearing God's word and putting it into practice (8:21). You will see how Luke holds the narrative together by use of repeated short summaries that help to keep you focused on the greatness of Jesus and on his bringing the kingdom (4:14–15, 44; 5:15; 7:17; 8:1–3). Also woven through the narrative, but not in a prominent role, is the beginning of opposition (5:17–21, 30; 6:7; 7:31–35, 44–49).

☐ 4:14–44   Good News for Nazareth and Capernaum

After an introductory summary (vv. 14–15), Luke uses Jesus' visit to the synagogue in his hometown of Nazareth to introduce the whole of his ministry (vv. 16–30)—fulfilling Old Testament promises; Spirit-empowered; with good news for the poor, including release of captives; justified by two Old Testament stories of the inclusion of Gentiles, resulting in opposition. Note especially that the opposition is the result of Jesus' reminding some Jews of God's prior inclusion of Gentiles (thus anticipating the story in Acts).

This is followed by two short narratives illustrating Jesus' powerful ministry on behalf of the poor and captives. Thus in his driving out demons and healing the sick (4:31–44), Jesus, the (humble) Divine Warrior, engages Satan in the holy war on Satan's own supposed turf (see 4:6; cf. 10:18).

☐ 5:1–6:11   Mission and Controversy

After calling his first disciples (5:1–11), Jesus' healing of a man with leprosy causes Jesus' fame to spread (vv. 12–16). It also sets up a series of conflict stories—on Jesus' right to forgive sins (vv. 17–26), his eating with sinners (vv. 27–32), his disciples' not fasting (vv. 33–39), and his breaking traditional Sabbath rules (6:1–11).

☐ 6:12–49   *Jesus Instructs His Disciples and Others*

Jesus now appoints the Twelve (Israel again!), whom he instructs (v. 20) in the presence of others (vv. 17–19) on the nature of discipleship. Note the emphases—on the humble poor, who are persecuted for Jesus' sake; on loving and not judging; and finally on obedience.

☐ 7:1–50   *Good News to the Poor*

Again Jesus shows compassion on the poor, in this case a Gentile (vv. 1–10), a widow (vv. 11–17), and a town prostitute (vv. 36–50). Note that the second story concludes with the exclamation that "a great prophet has appeared among us" (v. 16), which then leads to the narrative about Jesus and John the Baptist (vv. 18–35). Note further how the Pharisees' rejection of John (v. 30) leads to the final story in this section, where a view of the Pharisees emerges that will become thoroughgoing in the next section.

☐ 8:1–56   *Authentic Hearing, Fear, and Faith*

Luke now presents Jesus as a teacher of parables, so as to emphasize authentic hearing (the kind that leads to obedience, vv. 1–21). This is followed by three miracle stories (with four miracles), demonstrating Jesus' power over creation, demons, death, and uncleanness (see comments on Lev 11:1–16:34, p. 47). Note also how the first and last of these stories pick up the themes of *fear* and *faith*.

☐ 9:1–50   *The Identity of Jesus and Authentic Discipleship*

Watch for the significant role the Twelve play in this final series of narratives, beginning with Jesus' sending them out for ministry (vv. 1–9). The larger section then concludes with the confession of Peter and the first two predictions of Jesus' death (9:18–27; 9:43b–50), plus the transfiguration (vv. 28–36), where Jesus talks with Moses and Elijah about the "exodus" (vv. 30–31; see TNIV note) he is about to accomplish in Jerusalem.

On the Way to Jerusalem (9:51–19:44)

As you read this long travel narrative, you will find that even though the entire narrative is set "on the way to Jerusalem," that thread is often let go (among other things, the mission of the seventy-two and the events of two different Sabbaths are included). Luke probably intends us to read this section in light of the events already predicted, which are soon to transpire in Jerusalem. Also watch for several previous themes woven throughout: (1) the coming of God's salvation to all people, especially the poor and the lost; (2) regular, and sometimes harsh, confrontation between Jesus and the Jewish leaders; (3) the closely related theme that Jesus is going to Jerusalem to suffer and be killed; and (4) the formation of the disciples, especially preparing them for the time after his departure.

☐ **9:51 – 11:13** *Discipleship: Hearing and Doing the Word*

Notice how much of this material is aimed at instructing the disciples. Their attitude toward Samaritan opposition (9:51 – 55) is eventually challenged by Jesus' parable in 10:25 – 37, whose point is to demolish the question "Who is my neighbor?" Between these stand "the cost of discipleship" (9:57 – 62) and the mission of the seventy-two (10:1 – 24). Then comes the story of how one truly welcomes Jesus (vv. 38 – 42, by "listening to what [Jesus] said") as well as instruction on prayer (11:1 – 13).

☐ **11:14 – 54** *Opposition to Jesus*

In the next narratives, Jesus' authority is called into question first by some in the crowds over his driving out demons and then through their demanding a sign (vv. 15 – 16), to which Jesus responds in verses 17 – 32, and second by the Pharisees (vv. 37 – 38), to which Jesus responds with a series of woes on the Pharisees and their teachers (vv. 39 – 54).

☐ **12:1 – 13:9** *Discipleship and Preparedness*

Note the two emphases in this series of materials: (1) not pursuing wealth, but being content with what one has and being generous to the poor, and (2) vigilance in light of the coming eschatological crisis.

☐ **13:10 – 17:10** *Jesus in Opposition to Pharisaism*

You will see that this next series begins with a controversy between Jesus and the Pharisees over his showing compassion on the Sabbath (13:10 – 17). After two parables about the kingdom of God (vv. 18 – 21), he then responds to the question of who will be saved by implying that many will not (vv. 22 – 30), which in turn leads to his sorrow over Jerusalem (vv. 31 – 35). Following this, watch for two recurring themes in Jesus' conflict with the Pharisees—(1) their attitude toward the poor and the lost and (2) their attitude toward money (14:1–16:31). Note that the greatly loved parable of the prodigal son indicates that what is at stake between Jesus and the Pharisees is their opposing views of God (not a slaveholder [15:29], but a gracious, forgiving Father). The section then concludes with further instruction to the disciples on forgiveness and faithful servanthood (17:1–10).

☐ **17:11–19:27   *Responding to the Presence of the Kingdom***

Note how this final series begins with the reminder that Jesus is "on his way to Jerusalem." At issue is the proper response to the presence of the kingdom—thankfulness (17:11–19, involving a Samaritan again); faithfulness (17:20–18:8); humility (18:9–17); and the problem of wealth (18:18–30). After the third prediction of his coming death (18:31–34), Jesus heals a blind man and finds a lost man in Jericho (18:35–19:10). The final parable (19:11–27) is especially intended to prepare the disciples for his absence.

The Events of the End (and New Beginning) in Jerusalem (19:45–24:53)

☐ **19:45–21:38   *Jesus Teaches in the Temple***

As anticipated in chapters 1 and 2, Jesus now returns to the temple. After driving out the money changers, he takes his rightful place as teacher in the temple, an event which is set in the context of the religious leaders plotting to kill him (19:47). Note how this whole section thus portrays the conflict between Jesus and the opposition in the context of the temple, while "the people" (v. 48) play the role of learners who are on God's side. Note also how the parable of the tenants in the vineyard (20:9–19) makes it clear that the vineyard (cf. Isa 5:1–7) is about to be given over to others (Gentiles).

☐ **22:1–23:56   *The Trial and Death of Jesus***

Having shaped the narrative toward this point, Luke now recounts the events surrounding Jesus' death. Jesus is brought before three different tribunals (the Jewish Sanhedrin, Herod, and Pilate); note that before the political figures he is declared innocent of wrongdoing (23:4, 13–15). For the sake of his Gentile audience, who know that the Romans reserved crucifixion for slaves or noncitizen insurrectionists, Luke makes sure to note that Jesus himself "has done nothing to deserve death" (23:15). Even in his crucifixion, Jesus extends salvation to one of the "lost ones" (vv. 39–43)—who also affirms Jesus' innocence.

☐ 24:1–53 *The Vindication and Exaltation of Jesus*

Luke has the longest resurrection narrative among the four Gospels. Recognized in the breaking of bread, Jesus himself repeatedly interprets his death in terms of its divine necessity and prophetic fulfillment: Christ *must* suffer and rise from the dead, "and repentance for the forgiveness of sins ... be preached in his name to all nations, beginning at Jerusalem" (24:47), thus pointing to part 2 (Acts). Note that Luke concludes in the temple with rejoicing and waiting.

Luke's Gospel is one of the great treasures of the biblical story, emphasizing God's fulfillment of his promises to Israel—that "the year of the Lord's favor" (Luke 4:19) had come with Jesus' compassionate ministry of deliverance for and acceptance of the poor and helpless.

Acts

ORIENTING DATA FOR ACTS

- **Content:** part 2 of Luke's account of the good news about Jesus; how by the power of the Spirit the good news spread from Jerusalem to Rome
- **Author:** see the Gospel according to Luke
- **Date:** see Luke
- **Recipients:** see Luke
- **Emphases:** the good news of God's salvation through Jesus is for Jew and Gentile alike, thus fulfilling Old Testament expectations; the Holy Spirit guides the church in spreading the good news; the church has the good sense to side with God regarding his salvation and the inclusion of the Gentiles; salvation for all is God's thing and nothing can hinder it; the good news is accepted in joy by some and rejected in anger by others

OVERVIEW OF ACTS

In writing his larger account of the good news about Jesus, Luke has shaped the two parts to correspond in some significant ways. In Acts, for example, the geography is now reversed; it starts in Jerusalem and then branches out to other parts of Judea (chs. 1 – 12); its large central section is another travel narrative, as Paul takes the gospel from Antioch to Europe (chs. 13 – 20); the final third (chs. 21 – 28) portrays Paul's trials before the same three tribunals as Jesus (the Jewish Sanhedrin [Luke 22:66 – 71/Acts 22:30 – 23:10]; the Roman procurator [Luke 23:1 – 5, 13 – 25/Acts 24:1 – 27]; and one of the Herods [Luke 23:6 – 12/ Acts 25:23 – 26:32]) — which in Paul's case results in his getting the gospel to the heart of the empire (Rome).

The key to your reading of Acts is to recognize the "movement" of the gospel from Jerusalem to Rome, narrated in six parts (panels) and signaled by Luke's little summary statements in 6:7; 9:31; 12:24; 16:5; and 19:20. In each case the narrative seems to pause for a moment before it takes off in a new direction—sometimes geographically, sometimes ethnically, and sometimes both. The good news that is being spread, of course, is God's salvation (the forgiveness of sins) offered to all people (Jew and Gentile alike) through the death and resurrection of Jesus and by the power of the Holy Spirit. Here at last the promise to Abraham (Gen 12:2–3; see Acts 3:25), expressed repeatedly by the prophets as part of their hope for the future—that Gentiles would join Israel as the people of God (e.g., Isa 2:1–5; Mic 4:1–5; Zech 14:16–18)—had found its fulfillment.

The first panel (1:1–6:7) tells the story of the spread of the good news about Jesus in Jerusalem by the apostles. The second (6:8–9:31) marks the first geographical expansion to neighboring Judea and Samaria (see 1:8), where Stephen and the Hellenists play the major role. The third (9:32–12:24) narrates the first expansion to the Gentiles (Cornelius) and the conversion of the key figure (Paul) in what is to be its still greater expansion. With Paul now the central figure, the fourth panel (12:25–16:5) narrates the expansion to Gentiles in Asia, and how the early leaders dealt with the "problem" of Gentile inclusion "law-free." The fifth (16:6–19:20) marks the jump of the gospel from Asia to Europe; the church is also now steadily more Gentile than Jewish. The sixth (19:21–28:31) tells how Paul (the apostle to the Gentiles) finally got to Rome (the capital of the Gentile world) with the good news—but he did so, Luke reminds us, by way of Jerusalem through a series of trials very much like those of Jesus.

SPECIFIC ADVICE FOR READING ACTS

The story in part 2 is still about Jesus, as the brief prologue (1:1–2) reminds us. The first part was about what "Jesus *began* to do and to teach until the day he was taken up to heaven" (emphasis added). With some carefully chosen connections to part 1, Acts begins by picking up the prophecy from Luke 3:16 by John the Baptist about the coming Holy Spirit (Acts 1:5). The disciples are promised the "power" of the Holy Spirit (cf. Luke 24:49, "clothed with power from on high") so as to bear witness to Jesus. Luke then narrates the ascension (cf. Luke 24:51) in the context of Jesus' promised return; the clear implication is that through the Spirit they are to carry on the story until he comes (cf. the parable in Luke 19:11–27).

How Luke does this is the genius of Acts. First, note the large number of speeches that Luke records throughout the narrative (e.g., Peter in 2:14–39; 3:11–26; 10:27–43; Stephen in 7:1–53; Paul in 13:16–47; 17:22–31; 20:17–35). These tend to appear at key points and illustrate how the gospel is preached (or defended) in a variety of settings. In each case the speech either includes the essence of the story of Jesus or focuses on him at the end. Thus Jesus' story continues in Acts as the early believers bear witness to him.

Second, note (1) the connection between Jesus Christ and the Spirit and (2) that the Spirit is ultimately responsible for every major turning point in the narrative. How Luke connects Jesus and the Spirit is especially important. You will remember from reading Luke that the Spirit is the key to Jesus' earthly ministry (cf. Acts 10:38). Now "exalted to the right hand of God, he has *received* from the Father the promised Holy Spirit and *has poured out* what you now see and hear" (Acts 2:33, emphasis added). Christ, the great bearer of the Spirit, is also the great "baptizer" in the Spirit so that others will receive the Spirit and thus bear witness to Christ. It is therefore not surprising that at every turn, the Spirit is the driving force behind the forward movement of the gospel.

Third, because the gospel is God's thing, initiated by him and expressing his faithfulness to Israel through Christ, and carried out by the power of the Spirit, Luke also regularly reminds us that nothing can hinder it—not the Jewish leaders in Jerusalem (chs. 3–5; "you will not be able to stop these men; you will only find yourselves fighting against God," 5:39); not unbelieving Jews, like Saul of Tarsus, bent on destruction (8:1–3); not the church in Jerusalem (11:1–18; "who was I to think that I could stand in God's way?" Peter asks, v. 17); not secular leaders, like Herod (12:1–24, "Herod ... was eaten by worms and died. But the word of God continued to increase and spread"[!], vv. 23–24); not Judaizers within the church (15:1–35; "why do you try to test God?" v. 10); not religious or secular opposition from Greeks (16:16–40; 19:23–41); not shipwrecks or snakes (chs. 27–28). With the coming of Jesus and the Spirit, the time of God's favor has come. The gospel is God's activity in history; salvation is for all people, Jew and Gentile alike, and nothing can hinder it. And so the book concludes with Paul preaching in Rome with all boldness and without hindrance (28:31).

You will remember about Luke's Gospel that the universal nature of salvation was expressed in a *vertical* way to include the poor of every imaginable kind. In Acts Luke has concentrated *horizontally* on the Gentile mission—those ultimately marginalized by Israel. But throughout the narrative the restoration of Israel (Acts 1:6) is also always kept in view. The gospel begins as good news to Israel, "heirs of the prophets and of the covenant" (3:25), so that thousands turn to Christ from the start. As it moves outward, carried by Hellenistic Jews, it embraces fallen Jews (the Samaritans, 8:4–25) and a Jewish proselyte (8:26–40). The first Gentile convert is a "God-fearer" (10:2), and wherever Paul goes, he always begins in the synagogue, where some believe. And at the end, in Rome, he still pleads with Israel to believe in Jesus (28:17–28), but they refuse, so "God's salvation has been sent to the Gentiles, and they will listen!" (v. 28).

That leads us to remind you of the other side of Simeon's prophecy (Luke 2:34–35)—that Jesus will be a "sign that will be spoken against." You will want to note as the narrative progresses that the church becomes more and more composed of Gentiles, while Diaspora Jews and the Jewish leaders in Jerusalem lead the opposition. This obviously saddens Luke, but it also is part of the reminder to his implied (Gentile) readers that they belong to the Israel that God is reconstituting through Christ and the Spirit.

Finally, you will want to watch for the sudden insertion of "we" in the narrative at 16:10 (in Troas), which goes on until verse 17 (in Philippi), is picked up again at 20:5 (again in Troas), and continues through 21:19 (in Jerusalem) and again at 27:1 through 28:16 (from Caesarea to Rome). Two things are noteworthy about this phenomenon: (1) The author presents himself without fanfare as a sometime traveling companion of Paul, and (2) in these passages the details are far more abundant and vivid, suggesting that he may be using something like a diary.

A word about its placement in the canon. Luke understands his Gospel and Acts to be two parts of one story. It ended up in two books of about equal length (rather than one long book) because each would fit on one papyrus scroll. But in putting together the New Testament canon, the early church separated Luke from Acts (since both would have existed on separate scrolls, even when copied) through inspired insight. In the canon Luke now belongs to the fourfold Gospel, while Acts serves as a bridge between the Gospels and Paul. But in reading Acts, you need always to remember how it fits into Luke's inspired plan.

THE GOSPELS AND ACTS IN THE BIBLICAL STORY

A WALK THROUGH ACTS

☐ **1:1–6:7** *The Good News Begins in Jerusalem*

After the prologue that picks up where the Gospel left off (1:1–11), Luke first narrates the *filling up* of the Twelve (1:12–26), since they serve as the representatives of/to Israel. The coming of the Spirit then marks a new beginning (2:1–13; the Gentile world is already present in microcosm), followed by Peter's explanation of the phenomenon of tongues and the results (2:14–41). This is followed by a series of sketches that illustrate the early life of the church in Jerusalem—its common life (2:42–47; 4:32–37); its preaching and healing ministry (3:1–26; 5:12–16); the opposition (4:1–22; 5:17–42); and judgment within the community for "testing the Spirit" (5:1–11). What you will discover as you read is a new community that believes in Jesus but continues to live within Judaism.

Be looking also for two things that carry over from the last chapter of Luke's Gospel: (1) The disciples' ministry is primarily in the temple courts—the same temple courts cleansed by Jesus and made the arena of his final days of teaching (see Luke 19:45–21:38)—and (2) everything in this section is seen as fulfillment of very cardinal moments from the Old Testament story: the end-time gift of the Spirit promised by Joel (Acts 2:16–21); the resurrection of Jesus, as David's true heir (2:24–32); the present exaltation of Jesus as the exalted Lord of Psalm 110:1 (2:33–35); that the Messiah would suffer (3:17–23); that the promise to Abraham that he would bless the nations is about to be fulfilled (3:25); that the rejected Jesus is the rejected cornerstone of Psalm 118:22 (4:11) and the Messiah against whom the nations rage (4:25–26). Be on the watch for this motif as you continue through the rest of Acts.

The section ends (6:1–7) by noting that two groups have emerged within the community: Greek-speaking (Hellenistic) Jewish Christians and Aramaic-speaking (Jerusalem-based) Jewish Christians. The former of these, who belong to the Hellenistic synagogue in Jerusalem, become the key to the next expansion. Note how verse 7 brings this panel to a conclusion.

☐ **6:8–9:31** *The Good News Spreads to Judea and Samaria*

Note that this section picks up where the last one left off. You will see that the gospel has made significant inroads into the Greek-speaking synagogue (6:8–15). The first two of the leaders mentioned in 6:5 (Stephen and Philip) are responsible for the next phase of the story. Stephen's speech (ch. 7), patterned after such passages as Nehemiah 9:6–37 and Psalms 105 and 106, takes up the two crucial issues—from their accusation (Acts 6:13)—where the new wine cannot be contained in the old wineskins (Luke 5:36–39): (1) the temple (God does not dwell in buildings made by hands, in fulfillment of Isa 66:1–2) and (2) the law (the true lawbreakers are those who crucified Jesus, not the believers). Especially watch for the role of Moses in this speech—that he who was "rejected" by Israel (Acts 7:23–29, 35, 39) also foretold that God would send them "a prophet like me from your own people" (v. 37), who was also rejected (vv. 51–52).

Next comes the expansion to Samaria and to a Gentile proselyte through Philip's ministry (ch. 8); note here that Jesus is understood to be Isaiah's suffering servant (vv. 32–35). The panel then concludes with the conversion of one of the chief leaders of the opposition in the Hellenistic synagogue—Saul of Tarsus, who will be responsible (for the most part) for the next two phases of the expansion (Asia, Europe). Note how Saul is first introduced (8:1, 3); you might also want to look ahead to the two instances where Paul himself repeats this story (22:1–21; 26:2–23), in both cases emphasizing his role in the Gentile mission. Again, watch how 9:31 sums up and thus concludes this section.

□ **9:32–12:24** *The Good News Spreads to the Gentiles*

Note how Luke begins and ends this panel with Peter stories (9:32–43; 12:1–19). The first one is intended to set the stage for the Cornelius story and to remind you that the apostles continue to do mighty works. The conversion of Cornelius is so important that Luke narrates it twice (10:1–48; 11:1–18). The significance is that the first Gentile was brought to faith, not through the Hellenists (who might be suspect in Jerusalem), but through Peter, resistant though he is. The whole is orchestrated by the Holy Spirit. When criticized in Jerusalem, Peter tells the story all over again. Because of the work of the Spirit, Peter could not hinder God (11:17). Jerusalem is amazed: "even the Gentiles" (v. 18) get in on the good news. Also crucial to this panel is the founding of the church in Antioch by the Hellenists (vv. 19–30), since it will be the sending church for the mission to Asia and Europe. The Peter story with which the section ends (12:1–19) not only illustrates the "nothing can hinder it" motif but also sets the stage for the death of the opposition in this case (12:19–23). Note especially how the summary sentence of 12:24 sits in direct contrast to verse 23.

□ 12:25–16:5 *The Good News Spreads to Asia*

Look for several pivotal matters as you read this phase of the story: (1) The church in Antioch is the new center (12:25–13:3; 14:26–28); (2) Paul becomes the predominant figure (13:4–12); (3) the sermon in Pisidian Antioch (13:16–41) illustrates preaching in the Diaspora synagogues; and (4) the spread of the gospel also leads to the first open breach with Judaism, specifically over the Gentile mission, supported by Isaiah 49:6 (Acts 13:47).

Note how the three accounts in Acts 14 reinforce these themes, especially the power of God that accounts for the inclusion of many Gentiles and the widening breach between Diaspora Jews and the early believers in Christ. The Jerusalem council (15:1–35), with the chief roles being played by Peter and James, affirms a "law-free" gospel to the Gentiles. Note how brief the summarizing sentence is in this instance (16:5).

□ 16:6–19:20 *The Good News Spreads to Europe*

Here Luke records Paul's second and third missionary trips (16:6–18:22; 18:23–19:20); note how Paul always goes out from and returns to Antioch. The mission to Europe is especially orchestrated by the Spirit (16:6–10)—and here the author joins the story. In this panel Luke also records instances of conflict with pagan authorities (16:16–40; 17:5–9; 18:12–17), which tend to be instigated by Diaspora Jews (17:5, 13; 18:12). In each case the state either will not intervene or apologizes. Luke also includes here an example of preaching in a totally pagan environment (17:16–34). Again note how 19:20 functions to conclude the section.

□ 19:21–28:30 *The Good News (and Paul) Reaches Rome*

You should find this final section an absorbing narrative. As you read, don't miss that most of it deals with how Paul gets to Rome—through a series of trials similar to those of Jesus. Again be watching for the entrance and exit of the author. At the beginning and at the end, Paul is still reaching out to his fellow Jews (21:17–26; 28:17–28). But they resolutely reject Christ, so the final word is one of judgment in the words of Isaiah 6:9–10 (cf. Luke 8:10) and acceptance by the Gentiles (Acts 28:26–28). Note especially that in Paul's two "defenses" (22:1–21; 26:2–23), he tells his story so as to highlight his role in the Gentile mission. Also crucial to the story is the constant reminder that just as with Jesus (who, even though he died as a state criminal, had three times been pronounced "not guilty"), so with Paul: He and the church are found "not guilty" of wrongdoing against Rome (22:29; 23:26–30; 26:32).

In his vivid narrative of shipwreck in 27:1–28:16, Luke also makes it clear to us that Paul's getting to Rome was ultimately God's doing. So when the apostle to the Gentiles arrives in the Gentile capital, still reaching out to the Jews but affirming the Gentiles, Luke's grand story comes to an end.

It is hard to imagine how impoverished the biblical story would be without part 2 of Luke-Acts. Here we not only have a lot of the gaps filled in, but we are constantly reminded that the gospel is *God's thing* in the world—salvation for all through Jesus Christ and the Spirit.

The Gospel according to John

ORIENTING DATA FOR JOHN

- **Content:** the story of Jesus, Messiah and Son of God, told from the perspective of postresurrection insights; in his incarnation Jesus made God known and made his life available to all through the cross

- **Author:** the beloved disciple who "wrote [these things] down" (21:24; cf. 13:23; 19:25–27; 20:2; 21:7) most likely refers to John the apostle, son of Zebedee (otherwise not named in this Gospel); the "we" of 21:24 suggests another person is responsible for the Gospel in its final form

- **Date:** unknown; probably ca. A.D. 90–95

- **Recipients:** see 1 John, to which this Gospel is closely related

- **Emphases:** Jesus is the Messiah, the Son of God; in his incarnation and the crucifixion, he both revealed God's love and redeemed humanity; discipleship means to "remain in the vine" (Jesus) and to bear fruit (to love as he loved); the Holy Spirit will be given to his people to continue his work

OVERVIEW OF JOHN

John's Gospel is one of the great treasures of the Christian faith. Intentionally telling the story from a perspective after Jesus' resurrection and the gift of the Spirit (see 2:22; 12:16; 14:26; 16:13–14), John writes to reassure believers of the truth of what they believe (in light of defections and rejection)—that through the Incarnation God is fully and finally known. Here is God's love in full and open display.

In so doing, John puts the story of Jesus into the broadest biblical framework: The Incarnate One is none other than the Word, present with God from the beginning and responsible for creation (1:1–4, 10). But the Incarnate One is also the Crucified One, who, as God's Lamb, "takes away the sin of the world" (1:29). John is also concerned to demonstrate that the incarnate Son of God is in fact the long-awaited Jewish Messiah; thus Jesus bursts onto the world's stage, fulfilling every imaginable Jewish hope, while at the same time becoming "the Savior of the world" (4:42). Since he is the Son of (the living) God, what he gives is *life* (= the life of God himself)—eternal life (= the life of the coming age available now).

John begins with a prologue that puts much of this in poetic form (1:1–18), weaving theology and history together as he sets the stage for his telling of the story. The story itself is in two major parts (1:19–12:50; 13:1–20:31); it concludes with a commissioning epilogue and explanation of the (not-expected) death of the "disciple whom Jesus loved" (21:1–25).

In part 1 Jesus first manifests himself as Son of God to his disciples (1:19–2:11), who thus see "his glory" (1:14) and "put their faith in him" (2:11). He is then revealed to "the world" (2:13–12:50) as both the Messiah and the Son of God. John brings this off by telling the story in the setting of the Jewish feasts, where Jesus acts and speaks in ways that fulfill the rich messianic expectations expressed (especially) through the ceremonies connected with these feasts (Passover, 2:13–4:54; Sabbath, 5:1–47; Passover, 6:1–71; Tabernacles, 7:1–10:21; Dedication, 10:22–42; [prelude to the final] Passover, 11:1–12:36). Also in this section one finds the seven "signs" (John's *sign-ificant* word for miracles) and the seven "I am" sayings (Jesus' self-identification). Part 1 ends with a double conclusion, narrating first Jesus' rejection by some of the Jews (12:37–43) and then the meaning of Jesus and his mission (12:44–50).

The two narratives connected with the Passover (2:13–4:54; 6:1–71) also anticipate the final Passover narrated in part 2. Here the interest focuses first on the disciples as those who will carry on Jesus' mission (chs. 13–17) and then on the crucifixion itself (chs. 18–19), where the Son of God cries (triumphantly) about his work, "It is finished" (19:30). The narrative proper concludes with the resurrection (ch. 20), focusing especially on the commissioning of the disciples (20:19–23) and using Thomas's need to see as a foil for those who believe without seeing (vv. 24–31).

SPECIFIC ADVICE FOR READING JOHN

The thing that should most strike you when coming to John's Gospel from having read the Synoptics is how different it is. Not only is the basic scene of Jesus' ministry different (Jerusalem instead of Galilee), but the whole ministry looks quite different. Here you find no messianic secret (Jesus is openly confessed as Messiah from the start); no parables (but rich use of symbolic language); no driving out of demons; no narratives of the testing in the desert, the Transfiguration, or the Lord's Supper. Rather than placing emphasis on the kingdom of God, the emphasis is on Jesus himself (the Life who gives eternal life); rather than short, pithy, memorable sayings, the teaching comes most often in long discourses. As one scholar put it, "John seems to belong to a different world."

The reason is that John deliberately sets out to tell Jesus' story from the perspective of what he had come to know about him after the light had dawned (brought about by Jesus' resurrection and the gift of the Spirit). Moreover, John's interest in Jesus at his point in history (ca. A.D. 90–95) is shaped in particular by the false prophets who are denying the Incarnation and the saving significance of Jesus' death and resurrection, and who are marked by a failure to love others (see "Specific Advice for Reading 1 John," pp. 412–13). So part of the reason for his postresurrection perspective may be traced to this historical setting. You should note how often John emphasizes that Jesus is rooted deeply in flesh-and-blood history (he grows weary, thirsts, weeps at death; blood and water flow from his side while on the cross). The point is that the one whom John and his readers know as the exalted Son of God lived a truly human life on planet Earth and did so within the context of historical Judaism.

John's special perspective accounts for two other phenomena peculiar to his telling of the story—(1) the nature of many of his narratives and (2) the use of double meanings of words, closely related to the rich symbolism. You need to be ready to hear some things at two levels. John often starts with a narrative, which then evolves into a discourse—and at times you cannot tell where Jesus stops talking and John himself is interpreting (this Gospel is especially problematic for red-letter Bible editions!). For example, in 3:1–21 he starts with a straightforward narrative of Jesus' encounter with Nicodemus, but at its heart are wordplays on the Greek word *anōthen* (which can mean either "again" or "from above," which Nicodemus hears as "again" while John clearly intends both) and *pneuma* (the same word means "wind" and "Spirit"). And at verse 11 the "I/you [singular]" shifts to "we/you [plural]" and then moves into straight discourse, which from verses 15 to 21 comes in the language and style of 1 John. This has all the earmarks of Christian preaching, and it recurs throughout John's Gospel.

John's passion in this "preached" retelling of the story is threefold, two parts of which occur in his statement of purpose in 20:30–31. First, he cares especially to demonstrate that Jesus is deeply rooted in history as the Jewish Messiah, which is explicitly confessed by the disciples (1:41, 45; cf. 11:27) and confirmed by Jesus (4:25–26; 5:46; 10:24). Thus some of the "I am" sayings are full of Old Testament allusions— shepherd (Ezek 34), vine (Isa 5:1–7), bread (Exod 16:4; Ps 78:24)—where Jesus steps into the role of Israel itself (vine), as well as Israel's kingly Messiah (shepherd). Most significantly, John sets the entire story in the context of Jesus' being the fulfillment of Jewish messianic hopes associated with various aspects of the festival celebrations, matters often hidden to us but well known to him and his readers.

For example, at the Feast of Tabernacles there was a special water-pouring rite in the temple (described in the Talmud). This rite was related first to the giving of water from the rock in the desert (Exod 17:1–7); it came to be interpreted in a messianic way as pointing to the giving of the Spirit by the Messiah. It is on the "greatest day" of this feast that Jesus cries out, "Let anyone who is thirsty come to me and drink," which John then interprets in light of the gift of the Spirit (John 7:37–39). You are not necessarily expected to catch all of this as you read (a good commentary will guide you as to the details), but it is important to point out that there is often more than meets the eye in the reading of this Gospel. We will call your attention to some of this as you read along.

Second, John is concerned to demonstrate that Jesus, the Jewish Messiah, is none other than the Son of God (the Jewish messianic title from Ps 2:7 now understood as the Second Person of the Trinity). In Jesus, God himself has become present by incarnation. John takes every opportunity he can to press this point over and over again (cf. 1 John).

These two matters lead to the third—the "pathos" of the Gospel, which is to be found in Jewish rejection of their Messiah, precisely because of his claims to divinity. This emerges first in the prologue (1:10–13) and becomes a subtheme throughout the whole Gospel, but especially in 2:13–12:50. This is not anti-Semitism, as is often claimed (any more than when Jewish prophets even more fiercely denounced their fellow Jews for failure to follow God); rather it is expressed out of a heart broken over the failure of the people to follow their Messiah. Those who were best positioned to understand Jesus rejected him because they were unwilling to risk letting go of their own safe categories. But whatever else, John clearly believes that Jesus died for the Jewish nation, as well as for the world (11:51–52).

A WALK THROUGH JOHN

Prologue (1:1–18)

This wonderful passage you will want to come back to again and again. Here John emphasizes both the prehistorical and historical aspects of Jesus as the Word, the Son of God. Beginning with the Word before creation (vv. 1–2), John then tells of the Word's role in creation (vv. 3–5) and of the twofold response to his coming into the world (vv. 9–13), concluding with a confession (note the shift to the first-person plural) about his incarnation (v. 14) and deity (v. 18). Here also the *new exodus* motif begins: Believers in Jesus are the true "children of God" (cf. Exod 4:22–23), while Jesus is presented as greater than Moses (vv. 16–17), who led the first exodus. Interspersed is a contrast with John the Baptist (vv. 6–8, 15), which anticipates the beginning of the story itself.

The Messiah/Son of God Is Manifested to His Disciples (1:19–2:12)

Picking up from 1:1, John tells the beginning of the *new creation* in a seven-day scheme (five actual days; the last deliberately specified as three days after the fourth [2:1]), which in turn anticipates the seven days of the final week (12:1). What starts with the ministry of John the Baptist—some of whose disciples follow Jesus—climaxes at the wedding of Cana, where his disciples "put their faith in him" (2:11).

☐ 1:19–42 Days 1 to 3: Not John, but Jesus, Is the Messiah

Note how these first three days pick up the three things said about John the Baptist in the prologue (1:7–8): He was not the light (vv. 19–28); he came to bear witness to the light, in no less than four different messianic confessions (vv. 29–34); his witness was so that others—in this case, John the Baptist's own disciples—might believe in Jesus Christ (vv. 35–42). Note especially how this series ends with the confession by some of John's disciples, "We have found the Messiah."

☐ **1:43–51** *Day 4: Jesus Is Recognized by a True Israelite*

Watch for the ways this fourth day anticipates the *fulfillment of Jewish hopes* motif that pervades the rest of the story: A genuine Israelite without guile (playing on the name of Jacob ["he deceives"], Gen 25:26) confesses Jesus in the most Jewish confession in the Gospel ("Son of God ... King of Israel"; see Ps 2); he (and the others) will see the fulfillment of Jacob's ladder (Gen 28:10–22; "surely the LORD is in this place") come to pass in Jesus Christ.

☐ **2:1–12** *Day 7: Jesus Is Recognized As the Fulfillment of Jewish Messianic Hopes*

And now for the climax on the seventh day of the new creation: The best wine ("saved ... till now") is drawn out of six stone jars used for Jewish ceremonial washings! This outpouring of the best wine is seen by his disciples as fulfilling a significant aspect of Jewish messianic hopes (e.g., Isa 25:6; Jer 31:12; Amos 9:13–14). With this revelation of his "glory," the "first of his miraculous signs," his disciples "put their faith in him."

The Messiah/Son of God Is Manifested to the World (2:13–12:50)

In this section John places each of the narratives in the context of Jewish festivals; and in each case Jesus fulfills some aspect of messianic expectations associated with that feast.

☐ **2:13–4:54** *The First Passover*

In the context of Passover, John first narrates the temple cleansing, the significance of which lies at two points: (1) Jesus' actions divide the world into those who believe and those who do not, and (2) Jesus himself replaces the temple as the locus of God's presence (cf. 1:51).

This is followed by a series of four narratives (Nicodemus, John the Baptist, the Samaritans, the official's son), which continue motifs already in place—the exaltation of Jesus as Son of God in the context of some who do and do not believe (3:1–36); Jesus, not Jerusalem or Mount Gerizim, as the place of God's presence; and the confession of Jesus as "Savior of the world" (4:1–54). Note how the two narratives of chapter 4 also point toward the gathering of the nations—Samaria (vv. 1–42) and the "royal official" (vv. 43–54)

☐ 5:1–47   *An Unnamed Feast*

The next feast is unnamed because John's interest is in the *weekly* feast day, the Sabbath (5:1–47). The whole narrative assumes a Jewish belief that God continued to work on the Sabbath in three areas of his special divine prerogatives, namely, birth, death, and rain—all of which could and did occur on Sabbath days, giving evidence of God's "working" on the Sabbath.

Watch how John uses the healing of the invalid on the Sabbath as the basis for a discourse (vv. 16–47) on Jesus' assuming the divine prerogative of "work" on the Sabbath (giving life and judging [taking life]), which results in a confrontation with the Jewish leaders.

☐ 6:1–71   *The Second Passover*

As you read this second Passover narrative, you find Jesus functioning as the expected "prophet like [Moses]" (Deut 18:18) as he feeds the multitude and then offers them the bread of life. Playing on the Exodus theme of *bread from heaven,* which Jews expected to be renewed in the messianic age, Jesus offers himself as that bread, by offering them his "flesh" and his "blood" (John 6:48–58), thus anticipating the final Passover (chs. 13–20). Note that this feast ends with a winnowing of disciples.

☐ 7:1–10:21   *The Feast of Tabernacles*

For the Feast of Tabernacles John selects narratives where Jesus deliberately fulfills the three great symbols from Exodus celebrated in various ways during this feast in Jerusalem: (1) the water from the rock (Exod 17:1–7), (2) the light (pillar of cloud/fire) that guided the Israelites (Num 9:15–23), and (3) the giving of the divine name (Exod 3:13–15)—for background see especially Zechariah 14:6–9, 16–19. The concluding narrative—giving sight to a blind man (John 9)—illustrates how Jesus is the Light of the World. The Jewish leaders now threaten to put out of the synagogue any who confess Jesus as the Christ (vv. 22, 34). As you read the whole narrative note how Jesus is regularly the cause of division in Israel.

This narrative climaxes with the formerly blind man and the Pharisees standing in marked contrast with regard to Jesus (9:35–41), to which Jesus responds (10:1–21) by telling the Pharisees that he himself is the great messianic shepherd foretold by the prophet (Ezek 34:11–16, 20–31). Note how it ends (John 10:19–21): Jesus as the cause of division.

☐ 10:22–42 *The Feast of Dedication*

The Feast of Dedication celebrated the Maccabean restoration of worship in the second temple after it had been desecrated by Antiochus Epiphanes (see Dan 7–12); it was therefore a feast where Jewish patriotism and messianism ran high. Note how Jesus in this context presents himself—in the temple courts—as Messiah and Son of God, which again brings division in Israel: Some would now seize him (John 10:39); others believed in him (v. 42).

☐ 11:1–12:36 *Prelude to the Final Passover*

This prelude to the final Passover (note 11:55–12:1) is full of events and sayings that anticipate chapters 13–20—the climactic sign by the one who offers eternal life is the raising of Lazarus, which (ironically) will lead to Jesus' death, where God's glory is fully revealed; as the Resurrection and the Life (11:25), he both gives life and will raise his own on the last day; the high priest "prophesies" that one man will die for the Jewish nation and the "scattered children of God" (= Gentiles; 11:51–52); Jesus is anointed for his burial (12:1–11); he enters Jerusalem as their long-expected King (vv. 12–19); and to Greeks who want to "see Jesus" he responds by pointing to his exaltation on the cross (vv. 20–36).

☐ 12:37–50 *Conclusion: The House Is Divided*

Note that John now offers a double conclusion to Jesus' manifesting himself to the world (vv. 37–43, 44–50). You will not be surprised by now that the first one summarizes the mixed response to Jesus, as fulfillment of Isaianic prophecies. The second then summarizes what you have learned about Jesus in this section of the Gospel.

The Final Passover: The Messiah/Son of God Dies for the World (13:1–20:31)

Besides the narratives of Jesus' crucifixion (chs. 18–19) and resurrection (20:1–10), watch for John's special emphasis during this final Passover on the disciples, who will continue Jesus' ministry (13:1–17:26; 20:19–29).

☐ 13:1–17:26 *Jesus at Table with His Disciples*

In this long table talk, you will find Jesus repeating three themes over and over: I am going; you are staying to continue my work; but you can't do it alone, so I am sending you the Spirit.

Note especially how chapter 13 sets up the whole—Jesus' servant action that symbolizes his whole ministry (coming from heaven [he strips off his outer garment], he takes the servant's place in their behalf and calls them to follow him). Watch how the two major players in the next two scenes (Judas, who will betray Jesus, and Peter, who will deny knowing Jesus) are already presented in the first scene (vv. 2, 6–11).

Now see how the three main themes are emphasized in chapter 14: Jesus is going back to the Father, whom he has now fully revealed (vv. 1–10); they are staying to continue his works (vv. 11–14); he will return to them in the person of the Spirit (vv. 15–31). This leads to Jesus' applying Isaiah's vineyard parable (Isa 5:1–7) to himself and them (John 15:1–8), which leads to further expounding of the main themes (15:9–16:33), which now includes the world's hatred of them as the world hated Jesus.

Finally, Jesus' prayer (17:1–26) not only echoes these same themes but also anticipates the success of the disciples' mission to the nations—for whom Jesus also prays.

☐ 18:1–20:31 *Jesus: Slain and Raised Lamb*

Note how John's crucifixion narrative begins by narrating the fulfillment of the prophetic words from chapter 13—first Judas (13:18–30) in 18:1–14; second Peter (13:31–38) in 18:15–27. Thereafter John makes two special points: (1) Jesus is indeed the Jewish Messiah/King, but of a kingdom not of this world (18:28–40), and (2) Jesus dies at the same time as the Passover lambs (19:14), as he is "lifted up" on the cross (cf. 3:14–15; 12:32–33) to God's glory (cf. 11:4). His last utterance, "It is finished" (19:30), is a play on the word *fulfill* and thus has intentional double meaning: Jesus now dies; his death fulfills the work he came into the world to do.

The resurrection narrative then focuses especially on the disciples, leading to the commissioning. Note especially the significance of the Thomas narrative for the readers of John's Gospel: Thomas believed because he saw; blessed are those (John's readers, now including us) who believe on the basis of this Gospel, without otherwise seeing.

Epilogue (21:1–25)

After the beatitude and statement of purpose in 20:29–31, the epilogue focuses especially on Peter and the "disciple whom Jesus loved," with concern over the longevity of the life of the latter, but whose death has now either taken place or is imminent—before the coming of Christ. So the epilogue explains what Jesus really said in light of some apparent misunderstandings.

If the Synoptic Gospels care about Jesus' place in the history of Israel and beyond, John cares about Jesus' place in the whole scheme of things—from creation to redemption and beyond (final resurrection). That the Messiah is none other than the eternal Son of God is the ultimate good news of the Christian story.

The Epistles
and Revelation
in the Biblical Story

In our introductory chapter on the biblical story (see pp. 14–20), we noted the central role the people of God play in God's story (as the human "agonists"); we saw too that the "plot resolution" to the story is their redemption and reconciliation (with God and with one another).

The Epistles play a crucial role in the grand story, both defining how the plot resolution works out and how God's newly redeemed and reconciled people are to live in the present age, as they hopefully and joyfully await the final chapter of the story. Collectively, the Epistles presuppose the story of Jesus as told in the Gospels; their main concerns lie in the instruction, encouragement, and exhortation of God's people. As such, the Epistles share several things in common.

First, since the writers of the Epistles are primarily concerned with the salvation of God's people, Christ's death and resurrection play the absolutely key role in everything the writers say and do. At the same time, they also understand the role of the Spirit to be vital—as the way God and Christ are now present with God's people.

Second, all the Epistles are written to first-generation converts—even if sometimes after many years of living in the faith—and do not set out to give a full summary of Christian doctrine or ethics. As noted in *How to 1* (pp. 56–59), they are all ad hoc, written to specific situations in the lives of believers, most often in direct response to some false teaching that is circulating among the churches. This means that they tend to highlight those aspects of the gospel that expose and counter the errors they are combating.

Third, each of the Epistle writers lives and breathes an understanding of present existence that is eschatological (see *How to 1*, pp. 145–48). That is, they believe that with Jesus and the Spirit the time of the end has already begun and that they live between the times of Jesus' inauguration of God's rule and of his coming again to bring God's rule to full consummation. Thus, both the writers and the people addressed understand their new life in Christ to be "already" a reality but "not yet" what it will be at the end (1 John 3:2). By indwelling the individual believer as well as the gathered church, the Spirit is both the evidence that the future has already dawned (the down payment, or "deposit," Paul calls him, 2 Cor 1:22) and the guarantor of the final glory that is to be.

Fourth, the ethical imperatives (the supposed do's and don'ts) that occur throughout are not a new form of the law. Rather they are understood as expressions of God's own likeness as revealed in Christ (2 Cor 3:18; 4:4–6), and therefore they reflect what life in the final kingdom is to be like. The emphasis of the Epistles is that this life of the future is to be lived out now in the believing community as we await the final end. And here again the Spirit of God, who is now also known as the Spirit of Christ (Rom 8:9; 1 Pet 1:11), plays the central role.

About the Revelation of John: Although it functions as an epistle, it is in fact a word of prophecy expressed in the form of apocalyptic. As we point out in our chapter on the Revelation (see pp. 426–29), although writing primarily to encourage God's people in light of their soon-coming conflict with the Roman Empire over emperor worship, John at the same time gathers up strands of the story from both the Old and New Testaments and weaves them into a glorious tapestry of the final chapter of the story—so that the New echoes the Old in every imaginable way. When God's people live in God's eternal presence (Rev 21–22), the biblical story will have turned the final page.

In the meantime, don't forget as you read that this part of the story is ours as well. Here is where God writes us into his story. So read and enjoy.

Romans

ORIENTING DATA FOR ROMANS

- **Content:** a letter of instruction and exhortation setting forth Paul's understanding of the gospel — that Jew and Gentile together form one people of God, based on God's righteousness received through faith in Jesus Christ and on the gift of the Spirit

- **Author:** the apostle Paul

- **Date:** ca. A.D. 57, from Corinth (cf. Rom 15:25–26 with 1 Cor 16:1–7)

- **Recipients:** the church in Rome, which was neither founded by Paul nor under his jurisdiction — although he greets at least twenty-six people known to him (16:3–16)

- **Occasion:** a combination of three factors: (1) Phoebe's proposed visit to Rome (16:1–2; which would begin in the house church of old friends Priscilla and Aquila, 16:3–5), (2) Paul's own anticipated visit to Rome and desire that they help him with his proposed mission to Spain (15:17–29), and (3) information (apparently brought by visitors) about tensions between Jewish and Gentile believers there

- **Emphases:** Jews and Gentiles together as the one people of God; the role of the Jews in God's salvation through Christ; salvation by grace alone, received through faith in Christ Jesus and effected by the Spirit; the failure of the law and success of the Spirit in producing true righteousness; the need to be transformed in mind (by the Spirit) so as to live in unity as God's people in the present

OVERVIEW OF ROMANS

This letter is arguably the most influential book in Christian history, perhaps in the history of Western civilization. But that doesn't necessarily make it easy to read! While theologically minded people love it, others steer away from it (except for a few favorite passages), thinking it is too deep for them. But the overall argument and the reasons for it can be uncovered with a little spadework.

At issue is tension between Jewish and Gentile Christians in Rome, who probably meet in separate house churches and who appear to be at odds regarding Gentile adherence to the Jewish law—especially over the three basic means of Jewish identity in the Diaspora: circumcision (2:25 – 3:1; 4:9 – 12), Sabbath observance, and food laws (14:1 – 23). What is at stake practically is whether Gentiles must observe the Jewish law on these points. What is at stake theologically is the gospel itself—whether "God's righteousness" (= his righteous salvation that issues in right standing with God) comes by way of "doing" the law or by faith in Christ Jesus and the gift of the Spirit.

What drives the argument from beginning (1:16) to end (15:13) is expressed in the conclusion—that God might give Jews and Gentiles "the same attitude of mind toward each other that Christ Jesus had," so that together "with one mind and one voice you may glorify the God and Father of our Lord Jesus Christ" (15:5 – 6). The focus of the argument is on what makes such unity possible: God's righteousness given to Jew and Gentile alike on the basis of faith in Christ Jesus and effected through the gift of the Spirit. This primary issue is surrounded by matters having to do with Paul's hoped-for relationship with this church at the strategic center of the empire (1:1 – 15; 15:14 – 33), followed by a commendation of Phoebe (16:1 – 2) and greetings to friends (16:3 – 16), concluding with a final exhortation, greetings, and doxology (16:17 – 27).

The argument itself is in four major parts (1:16 – 4:25; 5:12 – 8:30; 9:1 – 11:32; 12:1 – 15:12), each of which concludes on a confessional note that also serves as a transition to the next part (5:1 – 11; 8:31 – 39; 11:33 – 36; 15:13). In turn the parts take up (1) the issue of human sinfulness, showing first its universality (Gentile and Jew alike, with the law offering no advantage to the Jew) and then the effectiveness of Christ in dealing with sin, so that right standing with God is based on faith alone—for which Abraham, the "father of us all" (4:16), serves as exhibit A; (2) how faith in Christ and the gift of the Spirit effect the kind of righteousness that the law intended but could not pull off, since it lacked the power to deal with human sinfulness; (3) how God is faithful despite Jewish unbelief, having a place for both Gentiles and Jews in the new "olive tree" (11:24); (4) what the righteousness effected by Christ and by the Spirit (thus apart from the law) looks like in terms of relationships within the believing community and beyond.

SPECIFIC ADVICE FOR READING ROMANS

The key to a good reading of Romans is not to get bogged down over the many bits of detail that beg for an answer. Rather, use "A Walk through Romans" to get the big picture, and then perhaps come back and, with the help of a good commentary, try to discover answers to its many pieces.

Knowing two things may help you as you read. First, the argumentation Paul employs in this letter is patterned after a form of ancient rhetoric known as the diatribe, in which a teacher tried to persuade students of the truth of a given philosophy through imagined dialogue, usually in the form of questions and answers. Very often an imagined debate partner (interlocutor) would raise objections or false conclusions, which, after a vigorous "By no means!" the teacher would take pains to correct.

You will notice as you read how thoroughgoing the diatribe pattern is. The imaginary interlocutor appears at several key places (2:1–5, 17–24; 8:2; 9:19–21; 11:17–24; 14:4, 10). Paul debates first with a Jew (2:1–5, 17–24), with whom he dialogues in most of the argument that follows, as he raises and answers questions and responds to anticipated objections (2:26; 3:1–9, 27–31; 4:1–3; 6:1–3, 15–16; 7:1, 7, 13; 8:31–35; 9:19; etc.). A Gentile interlocutor is finally introduced in 11:13–24. In both cases Paul begins by attacking ethnic pride (2:17–20; 11:18). Notice further how all of this is suspended when he comes to the exhortations that begin part 4 (12:1–13:14), only to be picked up again when the issue of Jew-Gentile relationships over food and days is brought to the fore (14:4, 10). Sometimes this form of argumentation can be dizzying, especially when in the course of it Paul makes some sweeping statements that may look contradictory. But in the end, all individual statements have to be kept in the context of the whole argument.

Second, the nature of the argumentation is such that it follows a logical sequence of ideas, but you should not think that this also represents a sequence of Christian experience (justification [chs. 1–5] followed by sanctification [chs. 6–8], as is often suggested). For example, even though the role of the Spirit is not examined thoroughly until 7:4–6 and 8:1–30, his role is already anticipated in 2:28–29 and 5:5. Likewise the inadequacy of the law is first presented in chapter 2, but in the context of the life of the Spirit it is raised again in 7:7–8:4 and hinted at again in 13:8–10. And what is said about the Spirit in 8:1–30 makes clear that his presence is presupposed in the argument of 6:1–14. Likewise the ethical specifics in chapters 12–14 presuppose the argument of chapters 6 and 8. The point is that Paul does not present the whole gospel at every turn; as you move forward in the letter, you will need constantly to try to keep the whole argument in view.

A WALK THROUGH ROMANS

☐ 1:1–7   *Salutation*

In this, the longest by far of his salutations, note how Paul already focuses on the gospel (vv. 2–4, to be resumed in vv. 16–17) as including the Gentiles (vv. 5–7).

☐ 1:8–15   *Thanksgiving and Prayer*

Watch how Paul's standard thanksgiving and prayer evolve into a narrative about his longing to come to Rome, a narrative that will be resumed in 15:14. Note especially how he backs away from pressing his apostolic status.

☐ 1:16–17   *The Thesis Stated*

As you read the rest of the letter, you will see how many of its ideas and concerns are anticipated in this thesis sentence (together with vv. 2–4): the gospel is about God's Son; it is God's power bringing salvation to Jew and Gentile alike; it is the revelation of God's righteousness, available to all on the same basis, namely, faith in Christ Jesus.

☐ 1:18–5:11   *Part 1: On Sin, the Law, Christ, and Faith*

Paul begins by painting the dismal picture of the human condition, starting with Gentile sinfulness: Idolatry leads both to the worship of the creature and to injustice and hatred of every kind (1:18–32). But note that he quickly counters by arguing that having the law does not thereby advantage the Jews, allowing them to judge others (2:1–11): (some) Gentiles who do not have the law do what the law demands (2:12–16) and (some) Jews who have the law still break the law (2:17–27). The only hope lies with *heart circumcision* (see Deut 30:6) by the Spirit (Rom 2:28–29).

After a brief (diatribal) look at the issue of God's faithfulness in light of Jewish sinfulness (3:1–8), Paul concludes with the bad news — that Jew and Gentile alike are sinful and need help, which the law could not provide (3:9–20).

God's own response is the greatest good news ever: Through the death of Jesus Christ, God's righteousness is given apart from the law and is available to Jew and Gentile alike by faith (3:21–26). Note how Paul then raises the three questions (3:27–31) to be answered in the rest of the argument: (1) "Boasting" is excluded; (2) its exclusion is based on the "law" of faith, apart from the Mosaic Law; (3) faith is the only answer, since there is only one God — for Gentiles as well as Jews.

For all of this Abraham serves as exhibit A (4:1–25). Note the emphasis that Abraham not only believed God and thus was credited with righteousness but also that this happened while he was still uncircumcised (a Gentile), thus making him the father of all, both Jew and Gentile alike (that is, those who believe God as he did, vv. 23–25).

Paul's response to this good news is to burst into confessional rhapsody, urging all his readers to enter into "peace" and to boast/rejoice in their hope and in their sufferings, since "we" have experienced God's love in Jesus Christ (5:1–11).

□ **5:12–8:39** *Part 2: On Sin, Christ, the Law, and the Spirit*

Note how part 2 begins as part 1 did, with the universal scope of human sinfulness. But now Paul goes back to Adam in order to point out the equally universal scope (= for Gentiles as well as Jews) of the righteousness made available in Christ (5:12–21).

Paul then takes up the issue of sins, given that sin itself is taken care of through the death and resurrection of Christ. Using three analogies — death/burial/resurrection pictured in Christian baptism (6:1–14), slavery and freedom (6:15–23), and death in marriage (7:1–3) — he concludes in 7:4–6 by urging that we die to the old (the flesh [sinful nature] and the law) and live in the new (Christ and the Spirit).

Since Paul has been so hard on the law to this point, he digresses momentarily to exonerate the law — it is God-given, after all — despite its role in our death (7:7–25). Lacking the Spirit, it stood helplessly by while "another law" — the sin that it aroused — took over and "killed" Paul (vv. 14–24).

God's response to this (8:1–30) is a *third law,* the Spirit (v. 2), who fulfills the law in us (v. 4) and stands against the sinful nature (vv. 5–13). The Spirit also leads us in the present (vv. 14–17) and guarantees the future (vv. 18–25), while aiding us in prayer in the midst of suffering (vv. 26–27) and conforming us to Christ's likeness (vv. 28–30).

Paul's response to all of this is the ecstasy of 8:31–39. God is "for us," not against us, in Christ, from whose love we can never be separated and in whom we are more than conquerors in all situations. Thus believers (especially Gentiles) don't need to go the way of the law.

□ **9:1–11:36** *Part 3: God's Faithfulness and Jewish Unfaithfulness*

Paul turns now to address the tension between God's faithfulness (in bringing Jew and Gentile together as one people) and Jewish unfaithfulness (in that the majority of Jews have not responded to the good news in Christ). The argument is in three phases, bookended by a lament over those of Israel who have rejected Christ (9:1–5) and a confessional conclusion, where Paul bows in praise and wonder before God's awesome sovereignty (11:33–36).

Note how the first phase (9:6–29) resumes the question of God's faithfulness from 3:3. Despite Jewish rejection, God's word has not failed; election needs to be understood along the new lines of a remnant and God's mercy on Gentiles.

Watch how the second phase (9:30–10:21), although still dealing with God's faithfulness, presents Israel's own responsibility for missing out on what God is now doing (with Gentiles now "in" and much of Israel "out").

The third phase (11:1–32) takes up the very tough question of whether God has rejected Israel altogether. Despite appearances, God has not cast off his ancient people; they have stumbled, but not totally fallen. Returning then to the concept of "remnant," Paul argues that God's new remnant people includes both Jew and Gentile; both have served, in different ways, to help bring the others in.

□ **12:1–15:13** *Part 4: The Practical Outworking
of God's Righteousness*

The (preceding) mercies of God call us to service of God, based on a renewed mind (by the Spirit) that can determine what pleases God (12:1–2). Note that verses 3–8 offer the basic theological grounding for the exhortations that follow: The believing community (of Jew and Gentile together as one body) is the arena in which all of this is to be worked out, first at the interpersonal level (vv. 9–21) and then in the world (13:1–7). Love is the linchpin (vv. 8–10), holding everything together (it fulfills the law and makes the rest of the argument work).

After pointing out to Gentile believers that the end of the law does not mean the end of righteousness (13:11–14), Paul concludes the whole argument on the very practical issue of Jew and Gentile respecting each other's attitudes toward food and days (14:1–15:13), urging each to accept the other (14:1; 15:1, 7). Notice how, in marvelous argumentation, he sides with the Gentiles theologically (14:17–18) but with the Jews practically (vv. 19–21). And note especially how the whole argument concludes in 15:5–8 with prayer and exhortation to "accept one another," followed by a series of Old Testament texts that include the Gentiles in God's story (vv. 9–12). The whole argument from 1:16 then concludes with the prayer of 15:13.

☐ 15:14–33 *Paul, the Gentile Mission, and Rome*

Picking up where the argument left off in 15:5–13, Paul points out his own role in bringing the gospel to Gentiles (vv. 14–22), which in turn leads him to lay out his plans to come to Rome—by way of Jerusalem (vv. 23–33).

☐ 16:1–27 *Concluding Matters*

The conclusion to the letter begins with a commendation of its bearer, Phoebe (16:1–2). This is followed in turn by greetings to friends in Rome (vv. 3–16), a final exhortation (vv. 17–20), final greetings (vv. 21–24), and a doxology (vv. 25–27). Note how at the very end Paul again stresses that it is in keeping with the prophets that "the Gentiles ... come to faith and obedience" (cf. 1:2–7).

Here God's story gets told in its primary theological expression. God's love for all, both Jew and Gentile alike, found expression in Christ's death and resurrection; the gift of the Spirit makes it all work out in everyday life.

1 Corinthians

ORIENTING DATA FOR I CORINTHIANS

- **Content:** a letter of correction, in which Paul stands over against the Corinthians on issue after issue, mostly behavioral, but which are nevertheless betrayals of the gospel of Christ and the life in the Spirit

- **Author:** the apostle Paul

- **Date:** ca. A.D. 53–54, from Ephesus (see 16:8)

- **Recipients:** the church in Corinth, composed mostly of Gentiles (12:2; 8:7)

- **Occasion:** Paul responds to a letter from the church (7:1) and to reports he has received (1:11; 5:1)

- **Emphases:** a crucified Messiah as the central message of the gospel; the cross as God's wisdom and power; Christian behavior that conforms to the gospel; the true nature of life in the Spirit; the future bodily resurrection of the Christian dead

OVERVIEW OF I CORINTHIANS

First Corinthians is the most difficult of the New Testament letters to summarize, because Paul deals in turn with no less than eleven different issues, sometimes in a length similar to some of his shorter letters (2 Thessalonians, Titus). Some items (on *divisions* and on *wisdom,* 1:10–4:21; on *incest,* 5:1–13; on *litigation,* 6:1–11; and on *going to prostitutes,* 6:12–20) are in direct response to reports from members of Chloe's household (1:11, probably an Ephesian Christian whose servants have been in Corinth on business). This may very well be true of the *head covering* of women in 11:2–16 as well and is almost certainly true of the *Lord's Table* correctives in 11:17–34.

The rest is in response to the Corinthians' letter to him mentioned in 7:1, where he starts by taking up the question of *sex and marriage* (7:1–24). At 7:25 the formula "Now about [virgins]" occurs, repeated in 8:1 ("Now about food sacrificed to idols"); 12:1 ("Now about spiritual gifts"); 16:1 ("Now about the collection"); and 16:12 ("Now about our brother Apollos"). Most of these are in direct response to behavior that is being embraced by some or most of the believers in Corinth; in each case Paul is *correcting* them, not informing them about things they do not yet know (notice how often he prods them with "Don't you know ..." where the implication is that they do in fact know; see 3:16; 5:6; 6:2, 3, 9, 15, 16, 19; 9:13, 24). The only issue raised that is not behavioral is the bodily resurrection of believers in chapter 15, and here Paul specifically says that "some of you say that there is no resurrection of the dead" (v. 12).

There is a degree of logic to the overall arrangement. He begins with matters reported to him (1:10–6:20), starting with the basic issue of divisions—within the community itself, but primarily over against Paul—before picking up other forms of breakdown in community relationships (incest, litigation, prostitution). Beginning at 7:1, he takes up issues from their letter, very likely in the order they occur. But when he comes to a couple of matters dealing with worship (attending idol feasts and the abuse of tongues), he inserts two other matters of worship that he has information about (head coverings and abuse of the Lord's Table). He puts the issue of the resurrection at the end of his response to Spirit giftings, because it probably reflects the false theology (or spirituality) that is responsible for the Corinthians' attitudes on most of the other issues as well. He concludes with more practical matters in chapter 16.

SPECIFIC ADVICE FOR READING 1 CORINTHIANS

To read 1 Corinthians well, you need some understanding of the city where the Corinthian believers lived. After lying dormant for nearly a hundred years, Corinth was refounded by Julius Caesar in 44 B.C. as a Roman colony. Because of its strategic location for commerce both north-south and east-west, by the time of Paul (one hundred years later) it had become the largest city in Roman Greece. By ancient standards it was a relatively new city, but it had quickly become cosmopolitan (having attracted people from all over the empire) and full of the *nouveau riche.* It was also very religious (all of the immigrants brought their deities), while at the same time morally decadent. So those who had become believers were from among this diverse population, both slave and free, Gentile and Jew (12:13), who brought a lot of their prior baggage with them to the Christian faith.

It is important as you read 1 Corinthians to be aware that the opposition to Paul in this letter (e.g. 4:3 – 5, 18 – 21; 9:1 – 2) was not from the outside — as in Galatians, 2 Corinthians 10 – 13, and 1 Thessalonians — but from within the church itself. A careful reading suggests that he and they (at least many of them) are at odds on every issue. They have either misunderstood or deliberately misinterpreted an earlier letter from him that prohibited certain vices (1 Cor 5:9 – 10) and have written to tell him why they think they are right and he is wrong (e.g. chs. 8 – 10; 12 – 14). And the conduct of some of them, which they have *not* written about, is so grotesquely unchristian that Paul is horrified that a Christian community could have brought itself to believe as they do. At times you can even pick out where Paul is citing them, often in agreement with their statement itself, but disagreeing with how they understand it (see 6:12 – 13; 7:1 – 2; 8:1, 4).

The primary place where he and they are at odds is over the question of *being spiritual* — what it means to be a person of the Spirit. This surfaces most sharply in chapters 12 – 15, where they apparently believe that speaking in tongues is to speak the language of angels (13:1) — they have thus already arrived at the ultimate state of spirituality, so much so that some of them have no use for a bodily resurrection (6:13 – 14; 15:12). This has also led to a triumphalist view of life in the present. Full of "wisdom" by the Spirit, they see Paul's weaknesses as evidence of a lesser spirituality (4:6 – 21). In such a view there is no room for the life of the cross. Hence the ease whereby they reject Paul's view on so many issues. Very likely their spirituality also lends itself to their low view of bodily activities (meaning they can indulge or be ascetic at will) so that some are even arguing against sexual life in marriage (7:1 – 7), and the traditional head coverings are being cast aside "because of the angels" (11:3 – 16, esp. v. 10).

Paul's basic response to all of this is to remind them that the gospel has a crucified Messiah, risen from the dead, at its very heart, and thus he bookends the letter with these two basic theological realities (the cross, 1:17 – 2:16; the resurrection, 15:1 – 58). Everything else in the letter must be understood in light of these; indeed, the most crucial role of the Spirit is to reveal the cross as the key to God's wisdom (2:6–16).

Because Paul sees the gospel itself at stake (especially because of the Corinthians' rejecting the centrality of the cross in Christian life), you will find his moods to run a wide gamut of emotion—confrontation (4:18–21; 9:1–12; 14:36–38), appeal (4:15–16; 10:31–11:1), sarcasm (4:8; 6:5, the "wise" aren't wise enough to settle disputes!), irony (1:26–28, no one in the name of wisdom would have chosen them to be God's people!), eloquence (13:1–8), and rhapsody (15:51–57)—but there is very little joy or pleasure to be found currently in his relationship with this church (and 2 Corinthians tells us it gets worse before it gets better).

A WALK THROUGH I CORINTHIANS

☐ **1:1–9** *Salutation, Prayer, and Thanksgiving*

Note how, typically, these formal elements are elaborated in ways that anticipate the rest of the letter ("sanctified in Christ Jesus"; "enriched in every way" [with Spirit giftings]). Significantly, Paul still thanks God for them—all of them—because they are God's people, after all, not his.

As you read the rest of the letter, look for the various elements of and reasons for the specific problems Paul is dealing with, and note now he responds to each.

☐ **1:10–4:21** *Divisions over Leaders in the Name of Wisdom*

The problem: a combination of (1) their anti-Paul sentiment, which (2) has broken out as strife over their leaders, which (3) is being carried on in the name of wisdom.

Paul's response: Note how he takes on the problem of wisdom first (1:13–3:4), urging that everything about the Corinthians' existence in Christ gives the lie to their present wisdom—the gospel of a crucified Messiah (1:18–25); their own calling (1:26–31); Paul's preaching (2:1–5). Indeed, one role of the Spirit is to reveal the cross as God's wisdom (2:6–16).

Second (3:5–23), he corrects their inadequate understanding of (1) leaders, who are merely servants (vv. 5–15), and of (2) the church, which is the temple of the living God in Corinth (vv. 16–17); thus there should be no boasting in mere mortals (vv. 18–23).

Third (4:1–21), he responds to their criticism of him: Since he is God's servant, they have no right to judge him; their pride reeks, so he appeals to them and warns them.

☐ **5:1 – 13   *A Case of Incest***

The problem: A believer is living incestuously with his "father's wife" (another wife of his father, but not his biological mother; see Lev 18:8); note that this is an instance where they are directly at odds with his previous letter to them (5:9).

Paul's response: Since Paul has already judged the offender, they are to gather in the power of Christ and turn him over to Satan (= put him back out of the church into Satan's sphere; cf. 1 Tim 1:20)—for the sake of the church in the present and finally for the offender's own salvation.

☐ **6:1 – 11   *External Litigation of an Internal Squabble***

The problem: One brother has cheated another (v. 8), who has taken him to the pagan courts for judgment (v. 1), and the church has done nothing (vv. 2–5).

Paul's response: Horrors! By doing nothing, the church has betrayed its existence as God's end-time people (vv. 2–4); shame on the litigant (vv. 6–7); warning to the defendant (vv. 8–10). But note how Paul ends by affirming their redemption through Jesus Christ and the Spirit (v. 11).

☐ **6:12–20   *On Going to the Prostitutes***

The problem: In the name of their rights as believers (v. 12) and on the basis of a low view of the body (v. 13), some men are arguing for the right to visit the prostitutes (understandable in light of 7:1–16).

Paul's response: Against *their* view of rights, only what is "beneficial" counts, and to be mastered by anything is a form of bondage (v. 12). Against their wrong view of the body, he appeals to the Lord's resurrection as affirming the body (v. 14) and to the nature of sexual intercourse as uniting two people (v. 15); one cannot thus be united to the Lord by the Spirit and united to a prostitute by sex (vv. 16–17), since the body belongs to the Lord as his temple (vv. 18–20).

☐ **7:1–24   *To the Married and Once-Married***

The problem: On the basis of a slogan, "It is good for a man not to have sexual relations with a woman," some women apparently (see v. 10) are arguing for no sex within marriage (because they have already assumed their "heavenly" existence in which there is no marrying or giving in marriage?), and if not regarding no sex, then for the right to divorce.

Paul's response: To the *already married* (vv. 1–7), stop depriving each other on this matter; instead, maintain full conjugal relationships. To *widows* and (probably) *widowers* (vv. 8–9), stay as you are. To the *presently married* (to a believing spouse, vv. 10–11), no divorce (= stay as you are). To the "rest" (= *presently married to an unbeliever,* vv. 12–16), do not seek divorce (= stay as you are).

The "rule" (vv. 17–24), based on God's calling and Christ's redemption is this: Stay as you are, since God's call sanctifies your present situation, but if change comes, that too is acceptable.

☐ 7:25–40   *To the Never-Before Married*

The problem: Based on the premise of 7:1, some are arguing that virgins (= betrothed young women) surely should not marry.

Paul's response: Note how Paul agrees with the conclusion but not the premise; hence he offers different reasons for staying single (the "present crisis"; unencumbered freedom to serve the Lord)—but whatever else, do not be anxious (v. 32), because marriage is also God's plan.

☐ 8:1–11:1   *On Idol Feasts and Marketplace Idol Food*

The problem: Since idols have no reality because there is only one God (8:4), some have argued against Paul that they should have the right to continue attending temple feasts (8:10), where all family celebrations were held; related is the matter of Jewish scruples about buying food once offered to an idol (10:23–11:1). They have apparently called into question Paul's right to forbid temple attendance—denying his apostleship on the basis of his not accepting their patronage (9:1–18) and his being wishy-washy about marketplace food (eating it in Gentile homes, but remaining kosher in Jewish homes, 9:19–23).

Paul's response: Note that Paul does not begin with a prohibition (that will come later; 10:14–22), but with their acting on the basis of *knowledge* (spiritual elitism again) rather than love (8:1–6). For most former idolaters the "god" had subjective reality, and being encouraged to return to the temples would destroy them (8:7–13).

Paul then (9:1–18) defends his apostolic right to their support, even though he has given that right up, and maintains that his actions regarding marketplace food are strictly in the interest of evangelism (9:19–23). After urging the need for self-discipline, with himself as a positive example (9:24–27), he warns them on the basis of Israel's negative examples (10:1–13). Finally, he explicitly forbids eating in the temples, since to do so is to participate in the demonic (10:14–22).

Turning to marketplace food itself in 10:23–11:1, Paul argues that Scripture itself makes clear that God doesn't care one way or the other—so buy and eat unless it bothers a pagan's conscience (someone who understands Christianity as a Jewish sect).

☐ 11:2–16   *On Head Coverings in Worship*

The problem: Most likely some women were discarding a traditional loose-fitting shawl on the basis of being as the angels, which apparently brought tensions in marital relationships (the women were, in their husbands' view, being like men).

Paul's response: Although women do have authority over their own heads on this matter (v. 10), in the Lord women and men are interdependent (vv. 7–9, 11–12), so the women should maintain the customs (vv. 13–16) so as not to appear like men (otherwise, he argues, go the whole way in looking like a man and be "shaved," vv. 5–6).

☐ 11:17–34   *Divisions at the Lord's Table*

The problem: Note that their division here is along the lines of rich and poor (v. 22) and is related to the eating of a meal in connection with the Lord's Table (vv. 17–21), at which the poor were being excluded (the church met in the houses of the well-to-do).

Paul's response: He reminds them of the words of institution (vv. 23–25) and that they must "discern the body of Christ" when they eat (= the church; see 10:16–17); otherwise they eat for judgment instead of blessing (11:27–32). Eat private meals privately; at community meals "make everyone equally welcome" (vv. 33–34).

☐ 12:1–14:40   *The Abuse of Speaking in Tongues*

The problem: Their view of tongues as the language of angels (13:1) caused them to overemphasize this gift in worship (14:18–19, 23), with the result that their community worship was nonintelligible and thus could not build up the body.

Paul's response: First, the primary criterion for Spirit utterances is the confession of Jesus as Lord (12:1–3). On the basis of their Trinitarian experience of God (vv. 4–6), Paul then urges diversity of giftings in the unity of the Spirit (vv. 7–31); in any case, love should rule at every point in their worship (13:1–13).

Pursuing love means first that only what is intelligible should occur in the community for the sake of edification (14:1–25) and second that everything must have a measure of order (vv. 26–40), because one's worship reflects what one believes about God's character (v. 33).

☐ **15:1–58** *The Bodily Resurrection of Believers*

The problem: Some are denying a bodily resurrection of believers (v. 12), apparently ridiculing the idea of a raised body (v. 35). Note that the placement of this issue in the letter suggests that it is closely related to chapters 12–14.

Paul's response: On the basis of Christ's resurrection, which they do believe (vv. 1–11), Paul argues for the certainty of our own resurrection (vv. 12–34), including (1) the folly of believing in the one and not the other (vv. 12–19); (2) both the inevitability (the firstfruits guarantees the final harvest) and necessity (death is God's final enemy to be overcome) of our resurrection (vv. 20–28); and (3) the senselessness of their actions, and of life itself, without such a hope (vv. 29–34).

As to "what kind of body," the answer is *the same, but not quite the same*—it will be spiritually refitted for heavenly existence (vv. 35–50). Notice how he concludes by taunting death in light of the certainty of our future (vv. 51–58)—here let your heart soar!

☐ **16:1–11** *On the Collection for the Poor*

The problem: Paul intends to take a substantial contribution from his Gentile churches to relieve the poor in Jerusalem; apparently the Corinthian believers have asked him about it.

Paul's response: Set some money aside weekly—to which he adds information about future plans, both his and Timothy's.

☐ **16:12–24** *Concluding Matters*

Note how he takes up their request for Apollos's return (v. 12) in a way that brings the letter to conclusion in typical style (staccato exhortations,

vv. 13–14; commendation of the letter's bearers, vv. 15–18; final greetings, vv. 19–24). But note also that here he adds a final curse and prayer (v. 22) and a word following the grace (v. 24, reassuring them of his love for them, given how strongly he has had to respond).

This letter holds an important place in the biblical story, reminding us constantly that (1) God calls a people to himself so that they might be conformed to his own likeness, reflected in the (apparent) weakness and folly of the cross, and that (2) in the end he will overcome our (and his) final enemy—death—by resurrection and/or transformation.

2 Corinthians

ORIENTING DATA FOR 2 CORINTHIANS

- **Content:** probably two letters (chs. 1–9; 10–13) combined into one, dealing primarily with Paul's tenuous relationship with the Corinthian church and in the process touching on several other matters as well (Paul's ministry, the collection for the poor in Jerusalem, and some Jewish Christian itinerants who have invaded the church)

- **Author:** the apostle Paul, joined by Timothy

- **Date:** ca. A.D. 54–55, from Macedonia (2:13; 7:5)—most likely Philippi

- **Recipients:** see 1 Corinthians

- **Occasion:** Titus's return from a recent visit (7:5–7) and Paul's anticipated third visit to the church (13:1) in light of (1) the church's need to have the collection ready before Paul gets there and (2) their readiness to embrace some "false apostles ... masquerading as apostles of Christ" (11:13)

- **Emphases:** Christian ministry as servanthood, reflecting that of Christ; the greater glory of the new covenant in contrast to the old; the glory of the gospel exhibited in the weakness of its ministers; the gospel as reconciliation; giving to the poor as an expression of generosity, not of obligation

OVERVIEW OF 2 CORINTHIANS

Reading 2 Corinthians is something like turning on the television in the middle of a very complicated play. People are talking and things are happening, but we're not at all sure who some of the characters are or what the plot is. In fact, in coming to this letter from 1 Corinthians, one has the sense of entering a new world. Few of the issues raised in the earlier letter appear here, except the concern over the collection (1 Cor 16:1–4/2 Cor 8–9) and perhaps a return to the matter of idol food in 2 Corinthians 6:14–7:1. But that is a surface view; what holds the two together is the overriding relational tension one senses between Paul and the Corinthians regarding true apostleship.

Four matters that play off against one another in the course of our letter(s) account for all of its parts: (1) Paul's change of plans regarding visits to Corinth, (2) the collection, (3) his apostleship and ministry, and (4) the presence of the Jewish Christian itinerants.

The first three matters carry over from 1 Corinthians and are dealt with in 2 Corinthians 1–9. A chronological explanation of his immediate past relations with them, apparently touched off by his change of mind about proposed and actual visits, is found in 1:12–2:13 and picked up again in 7:5–16. The long interruption of 2:14–7:4 is the crown jewel of the letter. Here Paul defends his apostleship-in-weakness (recall 1 Corinthians), a matter that has been aggravated by Paul's opponents (2:14–4:6). The need to have the collection ready before he comes is addressed in chapters 8–9. Chapters 10–13 contain a vigorous attack against his Jewish Christian opponents—comparable to that in Galatians (cf. Phil 3:2)—interspersed with indignation, biting sarcasm, and gentle appeals to the Corinthians to come to their senses.

SPECIFIC ADVICE FOR READING 2 CORINTHIANS

By any reckoning, you will find that 2 Corinthians is not easy to read, in the sense of seeing how it hangs together. Three things make it so. First, it is the most intensely personal of Paul's legacy of letters, made so because at issue throughout is Paul's ongoing, mostly painful, relationship with this church. The intensity of this personal dimension accounts for a number of things, including both the way Paul speaks and the difficulty we have at times in following the flow of thought (e.g., 2:14–7:4).

Second is the probability that 2 Corinthians is Paul's fourth and fifth letters to this church, joined as one in the transmissional process (a letter precedes our 1 Corinthians [see 1 Cor 5:9]; between 1 and 2 Corinthians there is the sorrowful letter mentioned in 2 Cor 2:3–4). There are two reasons for believing so: (1) Even though Paul speaks against the itinerants in 2:17–3:3 (those who "peddle the word of God for profit"), the rest of chapters 1–9 reflects a relatively stable situation, including appeals and terms of endearment (e.g., 1:7; 2:1–4; 6:11–13; 7:13–16), of a kind wholly lacking in 1 Corinthians. Almost everyone agrees that something has happened between his writing these words and what appears in chapters 10–13. (2) In 8:16–18 Paul commends Titus and another brother who will carry letter 4 (chs. 1–9) and pick up the collection; in 12:18 Paul refers to this sending as a past event.

Third is the question of how the four matters that make up the letter hang together. Our suggestion: Paul's relationship with this church, which was already tenuous when he wrote 1 Corinthians, had obviously soured. This is related in part to a change of plans regarding the itinerary outlined in 1 Corinthians 16:5–9. Instead of coming by way of Macedonia, he came directly from Ephesus, both to their great surprise and chagrin (the collection was not ready). A serious encounter with someone, alluded to in 2 Corinthians 2:1–2, 5–11, and 7:11–12 (perhaps one of the itinerants), caused Paul to leave just as abruptly as he had appeared.

In the meantime he changed plans yet again! Instead of returning to Corinth from Macedonia (1:15–16), he went on to Ephesus and sent Titus with his sorrowful letter (2:3–4), partly to make sure that the collection was under way (8:6). When he and Titus finally met in Macedonia (2:12–13; 7:5–7), Titus brought essentially good news. Even though Paul's letter had hurt them, as he knew it would, it had also led to repentance and (too much) discipline of the man who had attacked Paul (2:5–11). All of this is dealt with in chapters 1–7.

Paul's first reason for coming, however, is still in the forefront—to pick up the collection (chs. 8–9). Titus is thus being sent on ahead with letter 4 (chs. 1–9), which offers explanations for his actions and especially hopes to ensure that the collection will in fact be ready when Paul and some Macedonians come a bit later (9:1–5).

Meanwhile the itinerants were still plying their trade. By the time Titus arrived with letter 4, they appear to have gotten the upper hand, so Titus rushed back to Macedonia with the bad news, causing Paul to write again, this time confronting both the Corinthians and his opponents for their playing false with the gospel and with the true meaning of apostleship. This letter was preserved as chapters 10–13 of our 2 Corinthians.

In getting these matters into perspective for an easier reading of this letter, be sure not to lose sight of the grandeur of its theology, both of ministry and of the gospel. Here Paul picks up the theology of the cross as applied to ministry, which began in 1 Corinthians 4:9–13, and plays it out in full detail. God's glory—and the power of the gospel—is not minimized, but enhanced, through the weakness of the "jars of clay" (2 Cor 4:7; cf. 12:7–10) who proclaim it. Such ministry is in keeping with the Crucified One, after all. Hence Paul repeatedly glories in his weaknesses—not because he liked to suffer, but because it meant that attention was focused on the Savior, not on the messenger. And the passage dealing with the glory of the new covenant through Christ and the Spirit (3:1–18) is "worth the price of the book." So read, and enjoy!

A WALK THROUGH 2 CORINTHIANS

☐ **1:1–11** *Salutation and Praise to God*

Instead of the ordinary thanksgiving and prayer following a brief salutation (vv. 1–2), note in this case that Paul bursts into praise of God for comfort/encouragement in suffering (vv. 3–7), which serves as a way of bringing the Corinthians on board regarding his most recent escape from death (vv. 8–11).

☐ **1:12–2:13** *An Explanation of Paul's Change of Plans*

As you read this section, be alert to the fact that everything is in chronological order. So note that Paul feels compelled at the outset to give reasons for his most recent change of plans (1:12–17). This is because, at the end of the day, the gospel itself is at stake if its messengers are not themselves trustworthy (vv. 18–22). He then explains why he wrote the sorrowful letter instead of returning after the painful visit (1:23–2:4). After urging compassion on the man who caused Paul grief (2:5–11), resulting from his just-mentioned letter, he picks up with his itinerary from Ephesus to Troas to Macedonia, reflecting especially on his own anxiety over the sorrowful letter (2:12–13).

☐ **2:14–7:4** *Paul, Minister of the New Covenant*

Watch how Paul's anxiety with regard to receiving no news about Corinth in Troas results in this truly grand digression. Although the whole reads like a stream of consciousness, you can still trace how the stream flows. After an initial thanksgiving for victory despite present anxiety (2:14), he moves into wonder at his own God-given ministry (vv. 15–16), which he then sets in contrast to the itinerants, now in terms of the new covenant brought about by Christ and the Spirit (2:17–3:6).

This launches a contrast between the new and the old (3:7–18, evidence of the Jewishness of his opponents). To make some sense of this passage you might want to read Exodus 34:29–35, since this is a perfect example of what is known as a Jewish midrash—a sermonic application of an Old Testament text to a new situation. Note how it climaxes with the past work of Christ and the present work of the Spirit (2 Cor 3:14–18).

Paul then applies what has been said up to this point to his and their situation (4:1–6), which in turn leads to reflection on the tensions of living "already but not yet," contrasting present bodily weakness and suffering with eternal glory and future resurrection (4:7–5:10).

Returning to his own role in proclaiming Christ, Paul urges that Christ's death and resurrection change our perspective on everything—including how the Corinthians should view him and his sufferings as an apostle (5:11–17)—but note that mention of the gospel typically means elaboration of its glory and purposes, now (notably) in terms of reconciliation (5:18–21)!

Finally he appeals to them to accept both him and his gospel (6:1–2, 11–13), again set in a rhetorically powerful affirmation of present existence as "already but not yet" (vv. 3–10).

The unusual digression in 6:14–7:1 is probably over the issue of eating in the idol temples (cf. 1 Cor 8:1–13; 10:14–22), touched off by his appeal to openness regarding affection (2 Cor 6:11–13), to which he returns in 7:2–4, which finally brings him back to where he left off in 2:13.

☐ 7:5–16 *The Explanation Renewed*

Note how 7:5 picks up the chronological accounting of recent events from 2:13. Paul now explains how he has responded to Titus's return with the good news of their godly sorrow and generally open attitude toward Paul. He is especially pleased that Titus found them to be as Paul had boasted of them.

☐ 8:1–9:15 *Have the Collection Ready When I Come*

But for all their readiness to repent (7:11), there still remains the business that Titus could only begin (8:6) but not bring to completion, namely, the collection for the poor in Jerusalem. You will see that what now concerns Paul is that he has boasted to the Macedonians of the Corinthians' readiness, and some representatives of these churches are about to accompany him to Corinth (9:1 – 5). So surrounding the commendation of Titus and the two who will accompany him (8:16 – 24, Titus is to make sure the collection is ready), Paul appeals in turn to (1) the example of Macedonia (8:1 – 5), (2) their own excelling in so many things, including beginning the collection (8:6 – 12), (3) the biblical principle that those who have plenty should share with the needy (8:13 – 15), and finally (4) generosity as a true expression of godliness (9:6 – 15).

☐ 10:1 – 13:14 *Defense of Paul's Ministry against False Apostles*

Even though this issue is anticipated in 2:17 – 3:3, after the "sugar and honey" of 7:5 – 16 we are hardly prepared for the present barrage. You will see that the whole is a fierce defense of Paul's ministry, both personally and in terms of its character—all in light of the false apostles, whose slanders of Paul emerge throughout.

So Paul begins by taking one accusation of the opponents head-on— the alleged duplicity between his letters and his personal demeanor when with the Corinthians (10:1 – 11), pointing out in turn the opponents' duplicity of working his turf rather than evangelizing on their own (10:12 – 18).

This leads to a direct attack against them—they are deceitful purveyors of a false gospel (11:1 – 4)—followed by a scathing contrast between them (as servants of Satan, who take the Corinthians' money for their own gain) and himself (11:5 – 15). Personally ill at ease over what he feels he has been forced to do, he finally resorts to a "fool's" speech (11:16 – 33, the "fool" in the Greek theater enabled a playwright to speak boldly to his audience and get away with it). Since his opponents boast in their achievements (10:12 – 13; 11:18), Paul will "boast" in his *non*achievements, thus deliberately—and ironically—putting his ministry into a context of *conforming to the cross.* The ultimate irony is his escaping Damascus through a window in the wall (the highest honor in the Roman military was given to the first person to *scale* a wall in battle!).

He continues the boasting in weakness by refusing to give prominence to visions and revelations, as his opponents do, concluding on the ultimate theological note—that Christ's "power is made perfect in

[Paul's] weakness" (12:1–10), reflecting again the theology of the cross articulated in 1 Corinthians 1–4. This is followed by a series of (mostly personal) appeals (2 Cor 12:11–21).

The final exhortations (13:1–10) then sum up the preceding arguments before the final greetings (vv. 11–13)—and the ultimate Trinitarian benediction (v. 14).

The significance of this letter for the biblical story must not be downplayed because of its strongly personal dimension. At stake is God's own character—his loving grace expressed most strikingly in the weakness of the cross, which Paul insists is the only true expression of discipleship as well. Hence Paul's readiness to boast in his weaknesses, since they serve to magnify the gospel of grace, God's true power at work in the world.

Galatians

ORIENTING DATA FOR GALATIANS

- **Content:** a heated argument with the (Gentile) Galatian believers against some Jewish Christian "missionaries" who insist that Gentiles be circumcised if they are to be included in the people of God

- **Author:** the apostle Paul, joined by "all the brothers and sisters" with him (1:2)

- **Date:** probably ca. A.D. 55 (although some think as early as 47–48), with no indication of place of origin

- **Recipients:** Gentile believers in Galatia, either ethnic Galatians (whose territory in central Asia Minor had been earlier settled by people from Gaul [modern France]) or those in the Roman province of Galatia, which also included peoples of Pisidia, Lycaonia, and Phrygia (Acts 13–14; 16)

- **Occasion:** the churches of Galatia have been invaded by some agitators (5:12) who have questioned Paul's gospel and his apostleship; apparently some Galatians are on the verge of capitulating to them, which sparks a vigorous defense by Paul of his gospel and his calling

- **Emphases:** Paul's apostleship and gospel come directly from God and Christ, not through human mediation; the death of Jesus has brought an end to ethnic religious observances; the Spirit produces the righteousness the law could not; the Spirit enables believers not to yield to sinful desires; one receives the Spirit through faith in Christ Jesus

OVERVIEW OF GALATIANS

Like 2 Corinthians 10–12, this letter is clearly three-sided—*Paul*, to the *Galatians,* against the *agitators.* Paul is obviously red-hot (just like God in the Old Testament when his love for Israel has been spurned). Full of the Holy Spirit and in keeping with the nature of rhetoric under such circumstances, Paul writes with passion and forcefulness. Here you will encounter caustic and biting jibes at the agitators as well as fervent, sometimes cajoling, pleas to the Galatians not to give in to them. What could have inflamed such intensity?

The answer: The gospel is at stake, especially as it includes the Gentiles, law-free, in the people of God—not to mention Paul's own calling as apostle to the Gentiles. If the Galatians cave in to circumcision, everything God has done in Jesus Christ and is doing by the Spirit to include Gentiles in the people of God will have come to nothing (2:21). God's story itself is on the line.

Thus Paul comes out with guns blazing. First, he takes on the agitators' slander of his apostleship. In a series of three narratives, he starts by distancing himself from Jerusalem (1:13–24; his apostleship and gospel do not have human origins in any form), then points out Jerusalem's concurrence with him (2:1–10), and finally notes that any failure to keep the accord came from Jerusalem itself (2:11–14).

He then uses his speech to Peter on the latter occasion to launch his argument with the Galatians (2:15–21). The rest of the letter fluctuates three times between argument, application, and appeal (3:1–4:7/4:8–11/4:12–20; 4:21–27/4:28–31/5:1–12; 5:13–24/5:25–6:10/6:11–17). His *argument* is that the cross of Christ and the gift of the Spirit have brought observance of the Jewish law to an end. Notice how his *appeals* run the gamut, sometimes reflecting on past relationships (4:12–20; 5:7–10), sometimes pointing out the consequences of their proposed actions (4:8–11; 5:2–6), and sometimes disparaging the agitators (5:7–12; 6:11–13).

SPECIFIC ADVICE FOR READING GALATIANS

You may find the argument sections of this letter a bit hard to follow; this will be because of its "in house" nature, where Paul is arguing with the agitators on their own grounds. But with a little background knowledge you should be able to unpack it well enough.

Here is an instance where special vocabulary tells much of the tale. Note how often these key words occur: law 32*x*; flesh (TNIV 7*x* "sinful nature") 16*x*; works 7*x* (6*x* "observing the law," lit. "works of law"; 1*x* "acts of sinful nature," lit. "works of flesh"); circumcision/circumcise 13*x*; Christ 38*x*; the Spirit 17*x*; faith/believe 22/4*x*; grace 8*x*; justified/ justify 8*x*; Abraham 9*x*; promise 10*x*; son/seed 13/5*x*; freedom/free 4/6*x*; enslave/slave/slavery 11*x*; Gentiles 10*x*. While most of these words also occur in Paul's other letters, the number of times they appear in Galatians (and Romans as well) is out of proportion to their occurrences elsewhere.

At issue is the question, Who are the true *children/seed* of *Abraham* and thus true heirs of the *promises* made to Abraham? Paul's answer: Those, especially *Gentiles*, who have *faith* like Abraham's, who are thus *free*born *sons* and not *slaves*. They have become so by *faith in Christ* and the (promised) gift of *the Spirit;* on the other hand, those who would enforce Gentile believers to be *circumcised* are bringing them under the Jewish *law* and thus into *slavery. Justification* comes only by *grace;* to revert to *circumcision* is to seek advantage with God through *works of law,* which Paul sees as of the *flesh* (= ultimately putting trust in one's own achievements). All of this boils down to one basic matter: On what grounds are Gentile believers included in the people of God (= become part of Abraham's seed)? On their trusting Christ and their reception of the Spirit (their true identity marker), or by adding Jewish identity markers as well?

But why Abraham, you might well ask? Why not simply remind the Galatians of the story of Christ? The answer lies almost certainly with the arguments of the agitators, who have taken Genesis 17:1–22 as their primary text. There God established circumcision as "an everlasting covenant" in a context where Abraham was again promised to be the father of "many nations" (repeating the blessing of the Gentiles from Gen 12:3); in this context God promises that Sarah herself would bear a child, the legitimate heir—while Ishmael is already a young man. In all fairness, the agitators were not advocating a righteousness based on works; they had themselves put their faith in Christ. But, they would have argued, just as Abraham believed God (Gen 15:6) and then was given the covenant of circumcision, so the Gentiles who believe in Christ need to be circumcised in order to become the true children of Abraham, and thus heirs of the promise. At stake for them in the end is their own identity as the people of God, since the *marks of identity* for Jews in the Diaspora were especially circumcision, the food laws, and the sacred calendar, including Sabbath keeping.

Paul sees clearly where such an argument leads — to an equation that reads, "grace + works of law = favor with God." But adding a *plus factor* to grace in fact nullifies grace. Thus he argues that "grace + nothing = favor with God." Otherwise, believing Gentiles must in fact become Jews in order to be completed as Christians (3:3). Thus Paul appeals first to the Galatians' own experience of the Spirit (3:1–5) and then to Genesis 15:6 (which *precedes* 17:1–22 in the story), which says of Abraham that his *faith alone* was what God counted as righteousness (Gal 3:6–9). The rest of chapters 3 and 4 spell out various implications of these first two arguments. Paul shows first the preparatory and thus secondary nature of the law in relation to Christ and the Spirit (3:10–4:7), and then he shows that by rejecting Christ, the contemporary Jews have in effect made themselves the heirs of Ishmael rather than of Isaac (4:21–27). In any case their observance of the law is selective, and for Paul, to be under law means that one must observe the *whole* law (3:10; 5:3; cf. 6:13), not just parts of it.

The final argument (5:13–24) points out that the Spirit alone is sufficient for the kind of life in the present that reflects the likeness of Christ and stands over against the "desires" of the "sinful nature" (= flesh, referring to living in a self-centered way that is hostile to God) — which is precisely where the law failed. It could make people religious, but not truly re-formed so as to be shaped into God's own character (which is what the fruit of the Spirit reflects).

A WALK THROUGH GALATIANS

☐ 1:1–5 *Salutation*

Note how this unique salutation anticipates the argument by focusing on the heart of the gospel (vv. 4–5).

☐ 1:6–9 *A Curse on the Agitators*

You may find this paragraph abrupt, and for good reason, since this is Paul's only letter to a church that does not include a thanksgiving and prayer. Instead, he assumes the role of the prophet, pronouncing a double curse on those who are derailing the Gentile Galatians with a foreign gospel (and on any others who would do so).

☐ 1:10 – 2:14   *In Defense of the Gospel — Part 1: Paul and Jerusalem*

It is significant to note that Paul begins the defense of his gospel by defending his apostleship (which was a direct commission to take the gospel to the Gentiles). Thus, after a transitional sentence (1:10) against those who imply that by not insisting on circumcision, Paul is merely trying to please people, Paul begins by asserting that his gospel is not of human origin but came to him by revelation (vv. 11–12). The defense of this assertion then proceeds by way of a three-part chronological narrative — (1) that his gospel and apostleship (in contrast to that of the agitators) are absolutely *independent* of Jerusalem (vv. 13–24), thus capitalizing positively on what his opponents see as a negative; (2) that his gospel is nonetheless *in agreement* with Jerusalem and has their blessing (2:1–10, only spheres of ministry differ); and (3) that *Jerusalem* (in the person of Peter), not he, *broke faith* with the agreement (vv. 11–14).

☐ 2:15 – 21   *The Theological Propositions Set Forth*

Using his speech to Peter at Antioch as the point of reference, Paul makes the primary assertions about his gospel that the rest of the letter will argue — (1) that righteousness is "not by observing the law," (2) that righteousness is "by faith in Jesus Christ" (who brought law observance to an end), and (3) that the indwelling Christ (by his Spirit, of course) is the effective agent for living out the new righteousness (v. 20). Otherwise, Christ died for nothing (v. 21).

☐ 3:1 – 4:7   *In Defense of the Gospel — Part 2: Christ and the Law*

As you move now to Paul's theological defense of his gospel, note especially that it begins and ends with an appeal to his readers' experience of the Spirit (3:1–5; 4:6–7). The rest of this first argument is based on Scripture. The heart of it shows Christ's role in support of the first two propositions of 2:15–21: Having brought the time of the law to an end, he has ushered in the time of faith. Thus, Paul argues (in sequence):

3:7–9 — Abraham's true heirs are those who, like Abraham (and now including the Gentiles), have faith (in Christ Jesus).

3:10–14 — The law is not based on faith but on *doing*, which means doing the *whole law* (not just selected portions), which is also a "curse" because it excludes people from living by faith; thus Christ died so as to remove the curse so that Gentiles might be included by faith and through the Spirit.

3:15–18—Here Paul argues that the law, which came much later than the covenant with Abraham, is quite unrelated to the "promise" (that Gentiles will be included in the people of God—through the promised Holy Spirit) given to Abraham's "seed" (personified eventually by Israel's king, and thus finally realized in Christ).

3:19–22—Why then the law? It was added to *confine* God's people (keep them fenced in, as it were) until the promise was to be realized. And in any case, it was not intended to bring life, nor could it bring life (only Christ and the Spirit can do that).

3:23–4:7—The merely supervisory role of the law is over. Using the analogy of a child coming of age, Paul concludes (twice: 3:23–29; 4:1–7) that only faith in Christ Jesus produces true children/heirs, thus setting them free from slavery, through the gift of the Spirit (the Spirit of the Son, the true heir!).

☐ **4:8–20** *Application and Appeal*

In verses 8–11 Paul applies the preceding argument to his readers' specific situation. Since God *knows* them as his children, why go back to slavery? Notice the more personal, relational nature of verses 12–20, where he appeals to the Galatians to return to their earlier loyalty to him and devotion to Christ.

☐ **4:21–5:12** *Once More: Argument, Application, Appeal*

In 4:21–27 Paul returns to the scriptural argument of 3:6–4:7. By taking up the themes of Abraham, slavery, and freedom, he demonstrates by an analogy from Genesis that "doing the law" would mean slavery, while Christ and the Spirit mean freedom.

Note how this is followed by a threefold application and appeal. The Galatians are like Isaac, the free son of the "free woman" by "the power of the Spirit," and like Isaac, they are being persecuted by the slave woman's son, Ishmael—the Jewish Christian agitators (4:28–31). Again, note the personal nature of the appeals—(1) with a fervent call that the Galatians face up to the consequences of capitulating to circumcision, including their need to keep the whole law (5:1–6), and (2) with a scathing denunciation of the agitators, who have themselves abandoned faith in

Christ and are acting like a runner who cuts off others to keep them from winning (5:7–12).

☐ 5:13–6:10 *In Defense of the Gospel—Part 3:The Spirit and Righteousness*

Paul concludes by taking up the third proposition from 2:15–21—the indwelling Spirit has replaced law observance, because the Spirit can do what the law could not, namely, effect true righteousness (5:13–14, 22–23) and effectively combat the desires of "the sinful nature [flesh]" (vv. 16–21). Be sure to catch that this is set in the context of community disharmony (vv. 15, 26; note that eight of the fifteen "acts of the sinful nature" are sins of discord!). They are thus urged to live by the Spirit, who has brought them to life following Christ's death and resurrection (vv. 24–25). All of this is applied to very practical issues in 6:1–10.

☐ 6:11–18 *Conclusion: Circumcision No, the Cross Yes*

Paul concludes with another blistering attack on the agitators, who compel Gentiles to be circumcised but do not themselves keep the (whole) law (vv. 12–13), before turning the Galatians' attention once more to the cross (vv. 14–15). The final blessing (v. 16) is for all who live by the "rule" of verse 15 (circumcision is utterly irrelevant; only the new creation counts).

Because of the nature of the opposition, in this letter the basic lines of the truth of the gospel are most clearly drawn. Our understanding of the Christian faith would not be the same without this letter. Above all else, it serves as our own charter of freedom.

Ephesians

ORIENTING DATA FOR EPHESIANS

- **Content:** a letter of encouragement and exhortation, set against the backdrop of "the powers" (6:12), portraying Christ's bringing Jew and Gentile together into the one people of God as his ultimate triumph and glory

- **Author:** the apostle Paul (although many have doubts)

- **Date:** A.D. 61–62 (see "Orienting Data for Colossians," p. 359), probably from Rome

- **Recipients:** uncertain; perhaps a circular letter to many churches in the province of Asia, of which Ephesus is the capital (no city is given in the earliest manuscripts; Paul assumes the readers do not know him personally, 1:15; 3:2)

- **Occasion:** Tychicus, who is carrying this letter (6:21–22), is also carrying two letters to Colosse (Colossians and Philemon [Col 4:7–9]); perhaps after reflecting further on the Colossian situation and on the glory of Christ, and knowing the Asian fear of "the powers of this dark world," Paul writes a general pastoral letter for the churches of that area

- **Emphases:** the cosmic scope of the work of Christ; Christ's reconciliation of Jew and Gentile through the cross; Christ's supremacy over "the powers" for the sake of the church; Christian behavior that reflects the unity of the Spirit

OVERVIEW OF EPHESIANS

Writer and poet Eugene Peterson tells the story of his four-year-old grandson hopping up into his lap to hear a troll story. "Tell me a story, Grandpa," he begged, "and put me in it!" That is what Paul is doing in Ephesians, telling the ultimate story—God's story—and putting some Gentile believers—and us—in it (1:13–14; 2:13).

The churches of Asia Minor are in a period of difficulty. Some outside influences are putting pressure on Gentile believers to conform to Jewish identity markers (circumcision, food laws, religious calendar; see "Specific Advice for Reading Colossians," pp. 360–61). Others are discouraged, distressed by magic and the power of the demonic ("the spiritual forces of evil in the heavenly realms," Paul calls them, Eph 6:12), which had held them in their grip for so many years. As Paul is in prison thinking about these things and reflecting on the grandeur of Christ as expressed in his letter to the Colossians, his heart soars, and what he sees he writes down as encouragement for these churches.

You will hardly be able to miss the note of affirmation and encouragement in this letter. It begins with praise to God (in the form of a Jewish *berakah*: "Blessed be God") for the abundant blessings he has given in Christ (1:3–14); it carries on through the thanksgiving and prayer (vv. 15–23), into the narrative of Jew and Gentile reconciliation (2:1–22)—plus Paul's role in it (3:1–13)—and concludes with yet another prayer and doxology (3:14–21). The rest of the letter urges them to maintain the unity God has provided through Christ's death and resurrection and the Spirit's empowering (4:1–5:20), especially in Christian households (5:21–6:9), and concludes (6:10–20) by urging them to stand boldly in Christ and the Spirit and so to withstand the powers that are still arrayed against them (and us), while they (we) live in the present age.

SPECIFIC ADVICE FOR READING EPHESIANS

As you read you will want to be on constant alert for the three concerns that dominate the letter. The first is the passion of Paul's life—the *Gentile mission,* but not just the salvation of individual Gentiles. Rather, he asserts that by reconciling both Jew and Gentile to himself, God thereby *created out of the two a new humanity*—the ultimate expression of his redeeming work in Christ (2:14–16). This theme first emerges at the end of the opening blessing (1:11–14); it is developed in a thoroughgoing way in 2:11–22 and picked up again in 3:1–13. It is also this "unity of the Spirit" (between Jew and Gentile) that chapters 4–6 are all about by way of exhortation. Thus the whole letter is held together by this theme.

The second theme is *Christ's victory over "the powers"* for the sake of the church, with the Spirit playing the key role in our participation in that victory. You will see how Paul brings these first two concerns together early on in the letter—(1) in the "blessing" in 1:3–14, where Christ's redemptive, reconciling work embraces all things, both those in heaven (the "heavenly realms" are now his) and those on earth (Jew and Gentile as the one people of God), and (2) in telling them about his own role in the gospel (3:1–13), where the reality of Jew and Gentile together as the one people of God is on display before the powers so that they become aware of their present—and ultimate—defeat in Christ (vv. 10–12).

The first theme in turn lies behind the third concern as well, which makes up the second major part of the letter (chs. 4–6)—that they "walk" (4:1, 17; 5:2, 8, 15, usually translated "live" in the TNIV) so as to *maintain the "unity of the Spirit"* (4:1–16). This includes living out the life of Christ in their relationships (4:17–5:17), their worship (5:18–20), and in their Christian households (5:21–6:9)—those places where the worship would have taken place.

All three concerns are brought into final focus in 6:10–20, where, through the weapons and armor provided by Christ and the Spirit, Paul's readers are urged to stand as one people in their ongoing conflict with the powers.

As you read you will also want to note how Paul's Trinitarian experience of God lies behind everything. This comes out in the structure of the opening praise rendered to God: Father (1:3–6), Son (vv. 7–12), and Holy Spirit (vv. 13–14); note that each of these concludes with "to the praise of his glorious grace"; "for/to the praise of his glory." It is picked up again in the thanksgiving and prayer that follow (1:17), as well as in the narrative of reconciliation in 2:11–22, and serves as the basis for maintaining unity in chapters 4–6 (see 4:6–8; one Spirit, one Lord, one God and Father).

A WALK THROUGH EPHESIANS

☐ 1:3–14 *Praise to the Triune God*

Note that where he usually begins with thanksgiving and prayer for the recipients, Paul here begins with an opening "blessing" of the God who has blessed them through Christ and the Spirit. Besides being aware of the Trinitarian structure (as noted above), you should observe how Paul here introduces two of the major themes: (1) The Spirit's (TNIV "spiritual") blessings, provided through Christ, are theirs in the heavenly realms, the place of the habitation of the powers to whom they were formerly in bondage (v. 3), and (2) these blessings, especially redemption in Christ (vv. 4 – 10), have come to Jew and Gentile alike so that both together inherit the final glory of God (vv. 11 – 14).

☐ 1:15 – 23   *Thanksgiving and Prayer*

Here you find Paul's typical thanksgiving (vv. 15 – 16) and prayer (vv. 17 – 19). Notice how the prayer (for the Spirit's enlightenment) functions primarily to set the stage for the affirmations of his readers' present position in Christ, who presently sits at God's right hand as head over the powers for the sake of the church (vv. 20 – 23); note especially how this echoes the messianic Psalm 110:1.

☐ 2:1 – 10   *Reconciliation to God through Christ*

Flowing directly out of 1:20 – 23, Paul reminds his readers first of their past enslavement to the powers (2:1 – 3) and then of their present position with Christ in the heavenly realms, where he sits enthroned above the powers (vv. 4 – 7). Paul concludes with a kind of creedal statement: Life in the present is based on grace — not by "works" but for "good works" (vv. 8 – 10) — thus setting the stage for verses 11 – 22. You might want to read this section through and then read it again to see how much you can identify with the original readers.

☐ 2:11 – 22   *Reconciliation of Jew and Gentile through Christ and the Spirit*

This section, on the other hand, should keep us from reading verses 1 – 10 in a purely individualistic way. At stake for Paul is Gentile and Jew (and all other expressions of ethnic hatred) being joined together as the one people of God; they are made so, first, through Christ, whose death on the cross tore down the barriers that divide people, and, second, through the Spirit, who makes us one family as well as God's temple, the place of his present habitation on earth.

☐ 3:1 – 13   *Paul's Role in the Reconciling Work of Christ*

Note how Paul starts a prayer — picked up again in verse 14 — but interrupts himself to emphasize both his own role of proclaiming the "mystery" as well as the nature of the mystery itself, namely, that Gentiles are coheirs with Jews and therefore together with them form the one people of God, now especially as a reality on display before the powers—as evidence of their defeat!

☐ 3:14–21 *Prayer and Doxology*

Paul now prays that they—and we—might *experience* what he has just related, now in terms of knowing the *unknowable love of Christ* and thus to be filled, through the power of the Spirit, with all the fullness of God himself. Such prayer and its potential realization through the Spirit calls once more for praise to God (vv. 20–21).

☐ 4:1–16 *An Exhortation to Maintain the Unity (between Jew and Gentile)*

Note that narrative and prayer are now followed by imperative (words of exhortation). This is how Paul addresses his third major concern—that the Ephesian believers maintain "the unity of the Spirit" noted in 2:11–22. After giving the Trinitarian basis for it (vv. 4–6), he reflects on the gifts Christ has given to the church for its growing up into this unity.

☐ 4:17–6:9 *The Practical Outworking of Unity*

In this very important section you will find Paul now applying what he has urged in verses 1–16 to his readers' corporate and household existence as God's people in the world. They must give up their former way of life as Gentiles who lived in opposition to God (4:17–24). Notice that most of the sins mentioned next (vv. 25–31) are those that destroy harmony in human relationships; to continue in such sins is to give place to the devil (v. 27) and thus to grieve the Holy Spirit (4:30); rather they should walk in the way of Christ (5:1–2).

After a series of exhortations to abandon their former ways as Gentiles and become God's light in the darkness (5:3–17), Paul focuses on their corporate worship (which took place in the context of households). Thus the exhortation to "be filled with the Spirit" (5:18) for worship also serves as the hinge between relationships in general and within households in particular, where this worship would take place. After all, the Christian household was the basic expression of the Christian community.

Note especially that in the *household rules* (5:21–6:9), the householder himself (husband, father, master) is addressed in each case in relationship to the other three kinds of people in the household (wife, children, slaves). The key element in making the Christian household work is for the householder to "love [his wife], just as Christ loved the church and gave himself up for her" (5:25).

☐ **6:10–20** *Conclusion: Stand Strong against the Powers*

Paul concludes by urging his readers, in light of all that has been said to this point, to contend against the powers by means of the *armor* provided through redemption in Christ (vv. 13–17a) and the *weapons* of the Spirit (vv. 17b–20)—the word of God and prayer.

This letter is an essential part of the biblical story. It is clear that God takes the church far more seriously than some of his people in later times have done, precisely because it is the place where God has brought about reconciliation between diverse people, who were often bitter enemies, and made them his people who bear his likeness *in their life together*—and all of this as evidence that he has defeated "the powers."

Philippians

ORIENTING DATA FOR PHILIPPIANS

- **Content:** Paul's thanksgiving for, encouragement of, and exhortation to the suffering community of believers in Philippi, who are also experiencing some internal struggles

- **Author:** the apostle Paul, joined by his younger companion Timothy

- **Date:** probably A.D. 62, almost certainly from Rome

- **Recipients:** the church in Philippi (mostly Gentile), founded around A.D. 48–49 by Paul, Silas, and Timothy; Philippi is located at the eastern end of the vast plain of Macedonia on the very important Egnatian Way, which connected Rome with Byzantium (later Constantinople and Istanbul)

- **Occasion:** Epaphroditus, who had brought information about the church to Paul in prison and delivered their gift to him (2:30; 4:18), is about to return to Philippi, having now recovered from a nearly fatal illness (2:26–27)

- **Emphases:** Paul's and the Philippians' partnership in the gospel; Christ as the key to all of life, from beginning to end; knowing Christ, by becoming like him in his death (sacrificing oneself for others); rejoicing in Christ even in suffering; unity through humility and love; the certainty and pursuit of the final prize

OVERVIEW OF PHILIPPIANS

Philippians is the favorite letter of many Christians, full of wonderful and memorable passages. To his longtime friends at Philippi Paul bares his soul more than anywhere else in his letters (1:12–26; 3:4–14). Here you get a good look at what made Paul tick—Christ crucified and raised from the dead, whose story is recounted in 2:5–11. Paul has given up all his past religious "profits" and counts them as "loss," as "garbage," in comparison with knowing Christ, who is also the final prize he eagerly pursues (3:4–14).

But the community in Philippi is experiencing some inner tensions at the very time they are also undergoing suffering because of pagan opposition to their gospel, so Paul addresses this matter head-on (1:27–2:18). He also warns them against adopting Jewish marks of religious identity, especially circumcision (3:1–4), which would, in fact, make them enemies of Christ (3:18–19).

Thus even though Paul's and their "circumstances" make up the heart of this letter, everything finally focuses on Christ. Indeed, Paul urges the Philippians to follow his own example just as he follows Christ (3:15, 17; 4:9; cf. 2:5). Since the letter will be read aloud in church and since they are his friends no matter what, he saves his thanksgiving till the end (4:10–20)—acknowledging their gift with overflowing gratitude and reminding them that God himself accepted it as a sweet-smelling sacrifice (4:18), which leads to doxology (v. 20).

SPECIFIC ADVICE FOR READING PHILIPPIANS

Although Philippians is much loved, most people have a difficult time following its flow of thought, since it is not easy to see how everything fits together. Knowing three things should help you to see how the letter works and hopefully make it even more special to read—and obey!

First, friendship was a much more significant matter in the Greco-Roman world than it is in Western cultures, so much so that the highest level of friendship—between equals and based on mutual goodwill and trust—was the topic of several tracts among the philosophers, starting with Aristotle. Such friendship was entered into consciously, almost contractually. It was always accompanied by *social reciprocity* (that is, friends expected to "benefit" one another by their mutual goodwill and trust), which was most often expressed by way of metaphors from commerce, especially mutual *giving and receiving*. A striking feature of such friendship was the assumption that friends had mutual enemies, so that those who stood in opposition to one party in the friendship became the automatic enemies of the other (see John 19:12).

One type of ancient letter, the letter of friendship, arose out of this relationship; here the writer would share his or her own present thinking (often including reflection on one's circumstances) and inquire about the other's circumstances. Mutuality and goodwill always find expression in such letters, as do the obligations of benefits received and given.

That Paul had entered into such an arrangement with the Philippians (alone among all his churches) is explicitly stated in 4:14–16. All kinds of other features of friendship thus appear in Philippians—their mutual partnership in the gospel from the very beginning (1:3–5; 4:15); Paul's special affection for them (1:8; 4:1); Paul's enemies must also be theirs (3:1–4, 17–19). The whole letter fluctuates between his and their circumstances (the language referring to each other's circumstances, distinct to such letters, appears in 1:12, 27; 2:19, 23).

Second, another kind of letter was the letter of moral exhortation, usually written by the recipient's friend or moral superior. Such letters aimed to persuade or dissuade toward or away from certain kinds of attitudes or behavior. In such letters the author usually appealed to examples, including sometimes his own.

This is where the story of Christ in 2:5–11 fits into our letter, as well as Paul's own story in 3:4–14, whose point is that knowing Christ means to "become like him in his death." Those who do not follow Paul's example (3:17) are called "enemies of the cross" (3:18). These appeals are designed to curb the bickering that is going on in the community (2:1–4, 14; 4:2–3).

Third, the opposition to the church in Philippi is almost certainly related to the fact that Philippi was a Roman military colony. The town had been reconstituted by the first Roman emperor, Augustus (Octavian), and given to troops defeated and disbanded by him (at the battle of Philippi) during the Roman civil war. Because they had been thus favored by Octavian, the citizens of Philippi developed a fierce loyalty to the emperor as such. It is not surprising, therefore, that the cult of the emperor, with its devotion to the emperor as "lord and savior," flourished in Philippi. This loyalty brought its citizens into direct conflict with Christians and their devotion to Jesus Christ as the only Lord and Savior (cf. 3:20). Since Paul was also a prisoner of Rome because of the gospel (1:13), this meant that he and the Philippian believers were currently going through "the same struggle" (1:30).

This background makes it easy to think that part of the reason for the narrative of 1:12–26 is also to offer the Philippians an example of how to respond to such attempts to suppress the gospel, namely, to rejoice in the Lord and to determine, whatever the outcome, that "to live is Christ and to die is gain" (1:21).

As you read through the letter, see how often these things help you see how Paul is trying both to encourage and to exhort the Philippians to be like Christ, and like Paul his servant.

A WALK THROUGH PHILIPPIANS

☐ **1:1 – 11** *Salutation, Thanksgiving, and Prayer*

Because of his friendship with the addressees, in the (otherwise typical) salutation (vv. 1–2) Paul designates himself (and Timothy) as servants of Christ Jesus, rather than asserting his apostleship. Also, only in this letter does he mention "overseers and deacons" (v. 1, perhaps because two women leaders [4:2–3] were not seeing eye to eye on things?).

As usual, the prayer of thanksgiving (1:3–8) and petition (vv. 9–11) anticipates many of the concerns of the letter. You may wish to see how many of these you can spot as you read through the rest of the letter.

☐ **1:12 – 26** *Paul's Circumstances: Reflections on Imprisonment*

Paul begins by telling them how things are with himself (1:12–26): His own suffering at the hands of Rome has furthered the gospel through both friends and enemies, which is a cause for rejoicing in the Lord. The ground for such rejoicing is that Paul's life is not determined by circumstances ("life" or "death" in v. 20 means to be set free or executed), but by his relationship to Christ. Hence to "live" or "die" means Christ.

☐ **1:27 – 2:18** *The Philippians' Circumstances: Exhortation to Steadfastness and Unity*

The opening exhortation (1:27–30) sets out the two major concerns: (1) unity among the believers, in (2) a setting of opposition and suffering. The following appeal to unity and love (2:1–4) sets forth both the attitudes that destroy unity (selfish ambition and vain conceit) and that promote it (humility, putting others first), which is modeled by Christ.

Over against their attitudes and behavior he places Christ's self-emptying and his humility (by dying on the cross; 2:5–8). Before the ultimate Humble One, now exalted to the highest place, all human beings (including "lord" Nero), angels, and demons shall bow the knee and confess Christ's lordship (vv. 9–11). This is followed by further exhortations to "work out" their common salvation by not grumbling but rather by holding firmly to the word of life in Philippi (vv. 12–16). Note that the section concludes on a note similar to how it began—Paul's present suffering for their sake, with the invitation to joy (vv. 17–18).

☐ 2:19–30 *What's Next? Regarding Paul's and Their Circumstances*

Paul hopes to return to see his friends, but he is still in prison, so he will send Timothy as soon as there is news (vv. 19–24), and he is sending Epaphroditus now (vv. 25–30), who in God's mercy has recovered from his illness and is carrying Paul's letter to them.

☐ 3:1–4:3 *The Philippians' Circumstances Again: Warning and Appeal*

Since friendship also meant having *enemies* in common, Paul warns his friends one more time against those from "the circumcision," who would impose Jewish identity markers on Gentiles so as to "secure" them before God (3:1–3). This is simply "putting confidence in the flesh," Paul says, and that launches his own story (vv. 4–14). "Been there, done that," he says regarding such religious boasting; for him the heart and goal of everything is to know Christ now—by sharing in his sufferings—and to vigorously pursue the final prize of knowing him finally and completely.

All who truly follow Christ, Paul concludes, will see it this way, and as citizens of heaven they will finally be conformed to Christ's heavenly existence as well (3:15–21). Thus he returns one final time (4:1–3) to the earlier appeal to unity.

☐ 4:4–9 *Concluding Exhortations*

Although these are common to most of Paul's letters, note how the present exhortations are also shaped by the situation in Philippi (rejoicing in the Lord; being thankful; knowing God's peace, both in their hearts and in the community).

☐ 4:10–20 *Acknowledging Their Gift: Friendship and the Gospel*

In acknowledging their gift, Paul also returns to the theme of learning to live in the present with contentment, because he "can do all this [live in plenty or in want] through him who gives me strength" (vv. 11–13). But he concludes by bringing all the matters of friendship to a glorious

THE EPISTLES AND REVELATION IN THE BIBLICAL STORY

conclusion. With their ample supply toward his present needs, social reciprocity now lies on his side. But he is in prison and cannot presently *benefit* them, so he turns the matter over to "my God," who "will meet all your needs according to the riches of his glory in Christ Jesus" (vv. 14–19), which causes Paul then to burst into doxology (v. 20).

□ **4:21–23** *Closing Greetings*

These are especially brief in this letter, probably because Paul wants the words of verses 18–20 to be the final ones ringing in the Philippians' ears as the letter is read in church. But he does add a final encouragement by noting that among those sending greetings as followers of the Lord are members of "lord" Caesar's own household!

The whole of this wonderful letter is dominated by the story of Christ in 2:5–11, the Christ we are called both to serve and to be like. To "know Christ" means to live and act in the believing community as he did in his incarnation and crucifixion.

Colossians

ORIENTING DATA FOR COLOSSIANS

- **Content:** a letter encouraging relatively new believers to continue in the truth of Christ they have received, and warning them against outside religious influences

- **Author:** the apostle Paul, joined by his younger companion Timothy

- **Date:** probably A.D. 60–61 (if Paul is in Rome, as is most likely)

- **Recipient(s):** the (mostly Gentile) believers in Colosse (Colosse was the least significant of three towns noted for their medicinal spas [including Hierapolis and Laodicea] at a crucial crossroads in the Lycus River Valley, approximately 120 miles southwest of Ephesus); the letter is also to be read, as an exchange, in Laodicea (4:16)

- **Occasion:** Epaphras, a Pauline coworker who had founded the churches in the Lycus Valley, has recently come to Paul bringing news of the church, mostly good but some less so

- **Emphases:** the absolute supremacy and all-sufficiency of Christ, the Son of God; that Christ both forgives sin and removes one from the terror of "the powers"; religious rules and regulations count for nothing, but ethical life that bears God's own image counts for everything; Christlike living affects relationships of all kinds

OVERVIEW OF COLOSSIANS

Although Paul has never personally been to Colosse (2:1), he knows much about the believers there and considers them one of *his* churches—through his coworker Epaphras (1:7–8). His primary concern is that they stand firm in what they have been taught (1:23; 2:6–16; 3:1). After a glowing thanksgiving and encouraging prayer report (1:3–12), much of the first half of the letter reiterates the truth of the gospel they have received (1:13–22; 2:2–3, 6–7, 9–15). The rest of these two chapters exposes the follies of the errors to which some are being attracted (2:4, 8, 16–23). One may rightly guess, therefore, that the emphases in Paul's recounting the gospel are also there in response to the errors.

At the heart of the errors is a desire to regulate Christian life with rules about externals—"Do not handle! Do not taste! Do not touch!" (2:21, which sounds very much like certain forms of present-day Christianity). Most of chapters 3–4, therefore, take up the nature of genuinely Christian behavior. "Rules" and "regulations" have an appearance of wisdom, but no real value (2:23). Christian behavior results from having died and been raised with Christ (2:20; 3:1) and now being "hidden with Christ in God" (3:3), thus expressing itself "in the image of [the] Creator" (3:10). Note especially that the imperatives that flow out of these realities (3:12–4:6) are primarily directed toward community life, not toward individual one-on-one life with God.

SPECIFIC ADVICE FOR READING COLOSSIANS

As you read Colossians, you will want to be looking for four things. First, since so much that is said in Colossians is in direct (and indirect) response to some false teaching, be on the lookout for everything Paul says about these errors. Even though this matter does not emerge in a direct way until 2:4, by the time you are finished with chapter 2 you cannot help but see how important it is. Probably, therefore, much of what is said in 1:13–23 also was written with an eye toward what was falsely being taught.

Because of its importance for understanding this letter, a lot of scholarly energy has been devoted to the *false teaching,* trying to match it with what is otherwise known (or guessed at) in the Greco-Roman world. But at the end of the day all we know about it is what Paul says in this letter. We can't even be sure that there were "false teachers" as such; Paul's references are invariably to "anyone," "no one," etc. (2:4, 8, 16, 18). In any case, as you read, at least be looking for the various elements found in these errors.

The most obvious element is its Jewish flavor, which includes circumcision (2:11, 13), food laws, and the observance of the Jewish religious calendar (2:16); for Paul these are simply a written code standing over against us (2:14), merely "human commands and teachings" (2:22) that Christ has done away with. This element is apparently mixed with superstitions about angelic or spiritual powers (1:16; 2:8, 15, 18, 20), which seem also to have a powerful appeal both as divine "philosophy"— elite wisdom—(2:3, 8, 20) and divine "mystery" (1:26; 2:2). These teachings also seem to be in conflict with the physical side of Christ's earthly life and redemption (1:19, 22; 2:9).

Second, you will not be able to miss Paul's primary emphasis on the absolute *supremacy of Christ* over all things. This begins in 1:13, as the thanksgiving gives way to the exaltation of the Son, and carries through verse 22. It then recurs at every key point in the letter. Paul argues that Christ is the key to everything they need. All that God is ever going to do in and for the world has happened in and through him (1:19; 2:2–3, 9, 13–15, 20; 3:1). Paul also emphasizes the absolute supremacy of Christ over the powers, including Christ's role in creation and redemption. Christ is the whole package, so don't let go of him. He is the true "Head" trip (1:18; 2:10, 19).

Third, you will now want to think through the *situation in the church* one more time. Paul has never been there, but he has heard of their genuine faith in Christ. Notice the ways he tries to encourage them (1:3–12; 2:2; etc.), but note also the warnings (1:23; 2:4; etc.). At the same time think about how some things are said precisely because they do not know Paul personally but only through Epaphras. This is especially true of 1:24–2:5, where he sets his calling and ministry before them, especially in terms of the Gentile mission and what God has done through him by the power of the Spirit.

Fourth, at the end you may wish to read the whole letter again, this time with the knowledge that Onesimus (4:9) is being returned to Philemon for forgiveness, so Paul is preparing the church to *receive Onesimus* back as well (see Philemon). Read it at least once as you think Onesimus might have heard it; then perhaps try to put yourself in the shoes of a member of the church in Colosse.

A WALK THROUGH COLOSSIANS

☐ 1:1–2 *Salutation*

This is pretty standard, but note especially the emphasis on the Colossian believers already being holy and faithful.

☐ 1:3 – 14 *Thanksgiving and Prayer*

As usual, these anticipate much that is in the letter. The thanksgiving emphasizes the Colossians' already existing faith and love; the prayer asks for the Spirit's wisdom and understanding so that they might live lives worthy of Christ, made possible by God's power. Note how at the end the prayer gives way once more to thanksgiving (v. 12), which then trails off into a sentence that gives the reason for it—redemption through God's Son so as to share in his inheritance.

☐ 1:15 – 23 *The Supremacy of the Son of God*

This marvelous passage, which has a profoundly hymnic quality to it, actually continues the sentence that began in verse 12 (and continues through verse 16). Notice how what began with the Father's redemption through his Son, now proceeds to exalt the Son, who bears his image. In turn Paul proclaims first the Son's supremacy in relationship to the whole created order, including "the powers," as the creator of all things (vv. 15–17), and then in relationship to the church as its redeemer (vv. 18–22), concluding with a concern that the Colossians stay with Christ (v. 23).

☐ 1:24 – 2:5 *Paul's Role*

As you read this section, think about how it functions in a letter to a church that Paul has not founded or visited. His present imprisonment is to be understood as carrying on the sufferings of Christ for the sake of the (especially Gentile) church (1:24–27); his present role is to "strenuously contend" (an athletic metaphor) for members of churches like theirs and Laodicea, who have not known him personally, so that they might be encouraged and not fall prey to false teaching.

☐ 2:6 – 23 *Christ over against Religious Seductions of All Kinds*

Here you come to the heart of the letter. Christ in his incarnation and crucifixion both exposes and eliminates the "hollow philosophy" some are entertaining—a philosophy that first of all has to do with "the powers" (vv. 6–10). But note how in verses 11–19, this philosophy has been tied to an attempt to bring Gentile believers in Christ under the three primary identity markers of the Jewish Diaspora (see "Specific Advice for Reading Galatians," pp. 342–43), expecially food laws and the Jewish calendar (v. 16), and perhaps circumcision.

Note how Paul responds: They have received a new and truly effective circumcision—in the cross Christ has forgiven sin and triumphed over "the powers" (vv. 11–15); food laws and sacred days were a "shadow" of the reality, Christ himself, whose death and resurrection has forever eliminated the need to live by rules (vv. 16–23). Observe especially how Paul concludes: Rules "have an appearance of wisdom," but "lack any value in restraining sensual indulgence." Rules simply aim too low; believers are made for higher and better things.

☐ 3:1–11 *The New Basis for (Christian) Behavior*

Our participation in the death (2:20) and resurrection (3:1) of Christ eliminates the need to follow religious rules. Believers in Christ have died to those merely human things, having been raised to life by the one who is now exalted to the Father's right hand (see Ps 110:1). Paul then describes what we have died to (Col 3:5–9) and, by a shift of images (changing clothing), urges us to a life that reflects God's own image (v. 10). Verse 11 anticipates the imperatives that follow by reminding his readers that Christ has eliminated all cultural, religious, socioeconomic, and racial barriers.

☐ 3:12–4:6 *What Christian Life Looks Like*

Based on God's love and election (3:12), Paul proceeds to illustrate how God's image (in Christ) is to be lived out in their relationships with each other. Notice how everything flows out of the character traits of verse 12, two of which describe Christ in Matthew 11:29, and most of which are called "fruit of the Spirit" in Galatians 5:22–23. Remember as you read that these instructions in Christian behavior are *not* directed toward individual piety, but toward life in the Christian *community,* the basic expression of which is the Christian household.

☐ 4:7–18 *Final Greetings*

We learn much here, so don't read too hastily. Note especially the description of Onesimus (v. 9) as a "faithful and dear brother, who is one of you" (cf. Philemon). Note also how the greetings (Col 4:10–15) function to remind the Colossian believers that they belong to a much larger community of faith, including some mutual acquaintances.

What an important part of the biblical story this letter is, by its exaltation of Christ and by reminding us that behavior counts for something—but only as it is a reflection of Christ's own character and redemption.

1 Thessalonians

ORIENTING DATA FOR 1 THESSALONIANS

- **Content:** a letter of thanksgiving, encouragement, exhortation, and information for very recent Gentile believers in Christ

- **Author:** the apostle Paul, joined by his traveling companions Silas and Timothy

- **Date:** A.D. 50 or 51, while Paul is in Corinth, probably the earliest document in the New Testament

- **Recipients:** quite new converts to Christ in Thessalonica, mostly Gentile (1:9–10)—Thessalonica was a northern Aegean seaport that also sat astraddle the Egnatian Way (see "Orienting Data for Philippians," p. 353); in the time of Paul it was the chief city of Macedonia

- **Occasion:** the return of Timothy to Paul and Silas in Corinth; Timothy had been sent to Thessalonica to see how the new believers were doing (see 3:5–7)

- **Emphases:** Paul's loving concern for his friends in Thessalonica; suffering as part of Christian life; holiness regarding sexual matters; the need to do one's own work and not live off the largesse of others; the resurrection of the Christian dead; readiness for Christ's coming

OVERVIEW OF 1 THESSALONIANS

Put yourself in Paul's shoes. You have recently been to Macedonia's major city, where you had had good success in preaching the good news about Christ. But your success also aroused enormous opposition. Your host was arrested and charged with high treason, while friends ushered you out of the city by night so that you wouldn't be brought before the authorities. Thus your stay was much shorter than you had expected, and the new believers are now pretty much on their own, without a long period of seasoned instruction in the way of Christ. (See the account in Acts 17:1–9; the three Sabbath days mentioned in verse 2 does not mean that Paul was in the city for only that long. Rather that was how long he was able to work in the synagogue. Our letter indicates a church of much greater stability, Christian instruction, and renown than two or three weeks would have produced.)

So what would you have done? Try, as Paul did, to return, despite the danger (1 Thess 2:17–18)? And what if you could not return, because "Satan blocked [your] way"? And all the time you know nothing about what has happened in Thessalonica since you left (these were the days before postal service, not to mention telephone and e-mail service!). Very likely you would do what Paul did: Send a younger colleague, who could return without fear of being recognized or of suffering personal danger.

Now Timothy has returned to Paul and Silas in Corinth. A full half of our letter (chs. 1–3) is about Paul's past, present, and future relationship with these new converts, told in basically chronological fashion. Two clear things about Paul emerge in this section: (1) his deep, personal anxiety about the Thessalonians' situation and (2) his equally deep relief to learn that things are going basically very well (you can almost hear his sigh of relief in 3:6–8). Two things also emerge about the Thessalonian believers in these two chapters: (1) They continue to undergo suffering and persecution, but (2) they are basically hanging in there with regard to their faith in Christ—although there are also some things lacking.

The rest of the letter takes up matters that have been reported to him by Timothy. Most of them are reminders (see 4:1–2, 9; 5:1) of instructions they had been given when Paul and his companions were among them—about sexual immorality; mutual love, which includes working for one's own sustenance; and the return of Christ. One altogether new item is also included, namely, what happens to believers who have died before the coming of Christ (4:13–18).

SPECIFIC ADVICE FOR READING I THESSALONIANS

Keep in mind in reading this letter that it is most likely the earliest extant Christian document. To see how Paul deals with very new converts is part of the delight of reading. Notice especially how often Paul reminds them of things they already know (1:5; 2:1, 5, 9, 10, 11; 4:2, 9; 5:1). Given that Timothy's report about their faith was essentially positive and that on two matters Paul says there is no need to write (4:9; 5:1), the question is, Why then write at all? The answer lies in 3:9–10, where Paul thanks God that overall they are doing quite well, but that there are also some deficiencies. Since he cannot come now, he sends a letter as his way of being present and supplying "what is lacking in your faith."

On three matters (2:1–12; 4:1–8; 4:13–5:11) it is especially important to be aware of Greco-Roman culture in general and Thessalonian sociology in particular. First, every charge Paul defends himself against in 2:1–6 can be found in pagan philosophical writings—charges leveled against religious or philosophical charlatans. Almost certainly part of the suffering of the Thessalonian believers comes in the form of accusations against Paul (after all, he left town in the dead of night with political charges hanging in the air!). Second, the Greeks and Romans never considered immoral the kind of sexual behavior outside of marriage that both Jews and Christians saw as breaking the seventh commandment; what we would call sexual promiscuity—of all kinds—was simply an accepted way of life. Third, there is plenty of archaeological evidence indicating that the pagan Thessalonians were intensely interested in matters of life after death.

It is also of some interest to read 1 Thessalonians in conjunction with Philippians, since both are directed toward Macedonian (and therefore Greek) cities, yet their citizens are well known in antiquity for their loyalty to Caesar; in both cases Paul and the churches are undergoing persecution because of their loyalty to a "King" other than Caesar.

But there are differences as well. While 1 Thessalonians shows characteristics of a letter of friendship, that friendship was not of the more contractual kind Paul had with the Philippians. Note that in Philippi Paul had accepted financial support, whereas in Thessalonica, even though he stayed with Jason, he chose in this case to work with his own hands. This appears to mark a change in missionary strategy, which will serve Paul's theological interests in both Thessalonica and Corinth—here, because in 2 Thessalonians he will eventually appeal to his own example in order to reinforce the instruction given in 1 Thessalonians 4:9–12. See further the comments on 2 Thessalonians 3:6–15 on page 372.

A WALK THROUGH 1 THESSALONIANS

After the briefest of all of Paul's salutations (1:1), he begins with what turns out to be an extended "thanksgiving turned report" on their relationship (1:2–3:10), followed by a typical prayer report (3:11–13).

☐ **1:2 – 10** *Thanksgiving for Their Conversion*

Thanksgiving over the Thessalonian believers' faithfulness very soon gives way to a reminder of their conversion. Four things are stressed: (1) Paul's and the Holy Spirit's role in their conversion; (2) as with Paul—and in imitation of Christ—they experienced suffering in coming to faith, plus joy in the Holy Spirit; (3) news of their conversion had preceded Paul to Corinth (Achaia); (4) conversion included a turning from idolatry and a waiting for Christ's return.

☐ **2:1 – 12** *Recalling Paul's Ministry*

For their own sakes, Paul defends himself against charges of being a religious huckster. Notice that in verses 7–12 he uses three family images (infant, mother, father!) to refer to his relationship with them.

☐ **2:13 – 16** *The Thanksgiving—and Thessalonians' Suffering—Renewed*

Note how much this echoes 1:4–6. Here we also learn the source of their suffering ("your fellow Gentiles"), which reminds Paul of the source of his suffering (fellow Jews), whom he indicts for having crucified Christ and for trying to keep Gentiles from coming to faith (cf. Acts 17:1–8).

☐ **2:17 – 3:10** *Paul, the Thessalonians, and Timothy*

In successive paragraphs Paul picks up the narrative of his relationship with the Thessalonians since he (and Silas and Timothy) were "orphaned [!] ... from you for a short time." First (2:17–20), he reports on his own attempts to return and the reason for it; second (3:1–5), he reports on the sending of Timothy—to see how they were doing in light of their suffering; third (3:6–10), he expresses his great relief over Timothy's report "about your faith and love." All of this ends with a renewed thanksgiving.

☐ **3:11 – 13** *Prayer Report*

You should note that Paul prays for the very things he will now go on to speak about, namely, holiness, love, and the coming of Jesus Christ.

☐ **4:1 – 8** *On Sexual Purity*

Observe the clear shift here, as Paul moves on to pick up "what is lacking" in their faith (3:10). The first item is sexual immorality, reminding them that the God who called them and gave his Holy Spirit to them also calls them to a monogamous sexual life.

☐ 4:9–12   *On Love and Working with One's Own Hands*

Paul now moves on to the matter of mutual love—that some are not to be unnecessarily burdensome to others. On this matter, and the need to speak to it again, see 2 Thessalonians.

☐ 4:13–18   *On the Future of Christians Who have Died*

This paragraph reminds us of how brief Paul's time with them must have been. They had heard plenty about Christ's return (see 1:9–10; 5:1–11), but in the meantime, some of their company had died (because of the persecution?), and they simply didn't know what was to become of them. The answer: The dead will be resurrected; the living will be transported into the presence of Christ at his coming.

☐ 5:1–11   *On the Coming of Christ*

In light of the anxiety caused over the matter just addressed, Paul adds some encouraging words about the coming of Christ and his readers' participation in it. Although often read as warning, the passage is clearly intended to be an encouragement to a suffering community of believers (v. 11, "therefore encourage one another"). Since they are children of the day, they neither engage in nighttime activities nor should be caught by surprise at Christ's coming.

☐ 5:12–22   *Concluding Exhortations*

In turn Paul encourages respect/honor for leaders (vv. 12–13), urges healthy community relationships (vv. 14–15), exhorts basic piety (continual rejoicing, prayer, and thanksgiving; vv. 16–18), and prods them to encourage prophecy, but to test it and hold fast the good (vv. 19–22).

☐ 5:23–28   *Concluding Prayer and Greetings*

The prayer in particular recapitulates many of the items just addressed.

Here is a letter full of good things for the building up of relationships within the Christian community as we await the sure coming of our Lord, who will bring the present story to an end.

2 Thessalonians

ORIENTING DATA FOR 2 THESSALONIANS

- **Content:** a letter of further encouragement in the face of suffering, of warning against being misled regarding the coming of the Lord, and of exhortation for some to work with their own hands and not sponge off others

- **Author:** the apostle Paul, joined by his traveling companions Silas and Timothy

- **Date:** A.D. 51 (probably), very shortly after 1 Thessalonians (although some would reverse the order of our two letters)

- **Recipients:** see 1 Thessalonians

- **Occasion:** Paul has received word that some (probably by prophetic word) have spoken in Paul's name to the effect that the day of the Lord (= the coming of Christ) has already taken place, plus the fact that the disruptive loafers spoken to in 1 Thessalonians have not mended their ways

- **Emphases:** the sure salvation of the Thessalonian believers and the sure judgment of their persecutors; the day of the Lord is still ahead and will be preceded by "the rebellion"; those who are idle and disruptive should work for their food

OVERVIEW OF 2 THESSALONIANS

If you read this letter hard on the heels of 1 Thessalonians, you may notice that in general it lacks the warmth of feeling that you found in the first letter; and the material in 2 Thessalonians 2:1–12 is just obscure enough, especially in light of 1 Thessalonians 4:13–5:11, to cause you to wonder what gives. But what has caused the tone of this letter is easy to see. Both of the major items taken up (2 Thess 2:1–12; 3:6–15) give good reason for Paul to be upset—even more than he actually comes across as. In any case, the other sections of the letter (the thanksgiving and prayer in 1:3–12 and the prayer and request for prayer in 2:16–3:5) are full of the same kind of affection and concern Paul expresses in the earlier letter.

So what does give? First, Paul has learned from someone that the church is being thrown into confusion (2:2) by a declaration given in Paul's name that the day of the Lord has already happened. Both sides of this matter are enough to upset him—the falsehood itself and the fact that it is being put forward under Paul's authority. Since in 2:15 he tells them to hold fast to what he himself had taught them—by "word of mouth" (when he was present with them) and by "letter" (1 Thessalonians)—the problem in 2 Thessalonians 2:2 probably comes from an untested prophetic utterance (see 1 Thess 5:19–22) claiming to speak in Paul's name on this matter.

Second, he also has reason to be a bit miffed over those who are idle and disruptive, since he has already spoken to this issue in his first letter (1 Thess 4:9–12; 5:14).

Together these account both for the ambivalent tone and the specific content of the letter.

SPECIFIC ADVICE FOR READING 2 THESSALONIANS

For a brief letter, 2 Thessalonians has more than its share of difficult moments. First, although Paul expects certain events to take place before the coming of Christ (as you will see in 2:1–12), the specific nature of these events is less than certain. Most of our difficulty stems from the fact that at two crucial places (the identity of "the man of lawlessness" and "what is holding him back"), the Thessalonians had previously been informed, so Paul does not here repeat himself (2:5–6). Although these questions are obviously matters of interest for us as later readers, we will very likely have to be content to live with the main point of the passage, since we are outside the loop on these matters.

Second, there is also plenty of speculation—often given out as though it were plainly in the text—on the reason why the disruptive-idle continue not to work. The reason most commonly suggested is that they've quit working because they are expecting the soon coming of Jesus. But that hardly squares with what is actually being promoted in 2:2, that the day of the Lord has *already* come. More likely it is related to the general disdain of manual work on the part of Greek aristocracy. But nothing can be known for certain about the why; Paul's concern is, and ours should be as well, altogether with the *what*—both the exhortation to the disruptive-idle to get to work and the instruction to the church on how to treat such people.

A WALK THROUGH 2 THESSALONIANS

☐ **1:1–12** *Salutation, Thanksgiving, and Prayer*

Note several things as you read: (1) how the thanksgiving (vv. 3–10) affirms the Thessalonians in areas that need reinforcing; (2) that, as with 1 Thessalonians, it soon turns into narrative (vv. 6–10)—about the sure coming judgment of those who are persecuting them, while ending on the note of their own sure salvation—and (3) that the coming has a "can't miss the action" dimension to it (v. 7b), over against the teaching of those who claim it has already happened.

Watch how the prayer (vv. 11–12) then picks up the twin matters of faith and love from verse 3 (now in terms of deeds prompted by goodness and faith).

☐ **2:1–12** *Correcting Erroneous Teaching about Christ's Coming*

Paul begins the body of the letter (vv. 1–2) by urging the Thessalonian believers not to be shaken by the erroneous teaching (even though he is not quite sure of its source). As you read Paul's response (vv. 3–12), note first that he reminds them (vv. 5–6) of his earlier instruction on this matter to the effect that certain events must precede the coming of the Lord. Second, note how "the man of lawlessness" mentioned in verse 3 is the central figure in the whole narrative. A great rebellion will accompany his appearance (v. 4), effected in part by satanic miracles that dupe those who refuse to embrace the truth (vv. 9–12), but in the end he will be destroyed by Christ himself at Christ's coming (v. 8).

☐ **2:13–17** *Application and Prayer*

Paul next encourages the Thessalonian believers (vv. 13–14) by immediately setting them—those who have believed the truth and received the Spirit—in contrast to those mentioned in verses 10–12. He then urges them to stand firm in their former instruction (v. 15), finally praying both for their encouragement and their continuing faithfulness to Christian life and teaching (vv. 16–17).

☐ **3:1–5** *Request for Prayer*

Friendship in antiquity requires reciprocity (see "Specific Advice for Reading Philippians," p. 354); thus, having prayed for them in their present circumstances, he now asks them to pray for him in his.

☐ **3:6–15** *About Those Who Are Idle and Disruptive*

Before reading this section, you may wish to reread 1 Thessalonians 4:9–12. In returning to this matter, Paul uses himself as an example as he urges the disruptive-idle to work with their own hands so as not to burden anyone (2 Thess 3:6–13). Next (vv. 14–15), he tells the church what they are to do, namely, dissociate from those who refuse to obey, but always to think of them as brothers and sisters, not as enemies.

☐ **3:16–18** *Concluding Matters*

After passing the peace (v. 16), Paul takes quill in hand to sign off and thus guarantee the authenticity of the letter (v. 17), before the final grace-benediction (v. 18).

This letter fits into the biblical narrative as part of God's reassuring his people that Christ alone holds the key to the future and that they can trust him to defeat the enemy once and for all in his own time; in the meantime, love for one another also means not to impose on others' kindness.

1 Timothy

ORIENTING DATA FOR I TIMOTHY

- **Content:** an indictment of some false teachers—their character and teachings—with instructions on various community matters these teachers have brought to crisis, interspersed with words of encouragement to Timothy

- **Author:** the apostle Paul (although doubted by many)

- **Date:** A.D. 62–63, from Macedonia (probably Philippi or Thessalonica), apparently after his (expected) release from the imprisonment noted in Philippians 1:13 and 2:23–24

- **Recipient(s):** Timothy, a longtime, younger companion of Paul; and (ultimately) the church in Ephesus (the grace-benediction in 6:21 is plural)

- **Occasion:** Paul has left Timothy in charge of a very difficult situation in the church in Ephesus, where false teachers (probably local elders) are leading some house churches astray; Paul writes to the whole church through Timothy in order to strengthen Timothy's hand in stopping these straying elders and some younger widows who have followed them

- **Emphases:** the truth of the gospel as God's mercy shown toward all people; character qualifications for church leadership; speculative teachings, asceticism, and love of controversy and money disqualify one from church leadership; Timothy, by holding fast to the gospel, should model genuine Christian character and leadership

OVERVIEW OF I TIMOTHY

The letters to Timothy and Titus have long been called the Pastoral Epistles, under the assumption that they are intended to give instructions to young pastors on church order. But that tends both to read later concerns back into these letters and to lump them together in a way that loses their individual (and quite different) character and life setting. This letter is the first of the three, written soon after Paul had left Timothy in Ephesus. Having disfellowshipped the ringleaders of the false teaching (1:19–20), he left Timothy there while he went on to Macedonia, charging him to stop "certain persons [from teaching] false doctrines any longer" (1:3).

The letter fluctuates between words to the *church* through Timothy and words to *Timothy* himself, although even these latter are intended to be overheard by the church. Much of the letter points out the follies of the false teachers/teaching (1:4–10, 19b–20; 4:1–3, 7; 6:3–10, 20–21). The words to Timothy (1:3, 18–19a; 4:6–16; 6:11–16, 20–21) charge him with regard to his duties and encourage him and strengthen his hand before the community to carry out these (sometimes unpleasant) duties. These two matters merge in the final charge to Timothy in 6:20–21. The rest of the letter deals with community matters, obviously deeply influenced by the false teaching—matters such as the believers' gathering for prayer and teaching (2:1–15); qualifications for, and replacement of, leaders (3:1–13; 5:17–25); caring for older widows, but urging younger ones to marry (5:3–16); attitudes of slaves toward masters (6:1–2).

Despite the many words directed personally to Timothy, this letter is all business, as is made clear by a lack of both the ordinary thanksgiving and prayer reports that begin Paul's letters (cf. 2 Timothy) and the greetings to and from friends that conclude them (again, cf. 2 Timothy).

SPECIFIC ADVICE FOR READING I TIMOTHY

As you read, note especially what Paul says about the false teachers and their teaching—since concern about them appears to lie behind every word in this letter. There are good reasons to assume that these teachers were local elders who had embraced some ideas that are quite incompatible with the gospel of grace (1:11–17): First, unlike the other letters of Paul that deal with false teachers (2 Corinthians, Galatians, Philippians), 1 Timothy gives no hint that these teachers might be outsiders. Second, Paul has already excommunicated two of them, clearly insiders (1 Tim 1:19–20), and the later evidence from 2 Timothy 2:17–18 indicates that one of them (Hymenaeus) refused to leave (note that he is named first both times, implying that he is the ringleader). Now, third, read Paul's address to the elders of this church in Acts 20:17–35, and note that, some five years or so earlier, Paul had predicted this very thing would happen (vv. 29–30, that from among their own number some would arise and distort the truth).

If you add one additional factor, that these elders have made use of some younger widows who have opened their homes to their novelties — as 2 Timothy 3:6–7 states — then the whole letter falls into place. Note how these factors together explain (1) why Paul writes to Timothy, and not to the church as in other such cases, since his letter would not get a hearing in the hands of these elders; at the same time Paul is authorizing Timothy before the church to see that these elders are replaced by people with proper qualifications; (2) why he gives careful instructions, not about the duties of elders, but about their qualifications; (3) why he gives such detailed instructions about caring for older widows, while urging the younger ones, some of whom have already gone astray after Satan (1 Tim 5:15), to marry — against his general advice in 1 Corinthians 7:40 — and why he forbids them to teach in this setting (1 Tim 2:11–15); and (4) why, although his primary concern is for the gospel (1:11), Paul gives so little of its content in this letter — since Timothy does not need instruction here — and why on the other hand so much is said about the nature of the false teaching.

The false teaching seems to be a mixture of things Jewish and Greek. Errantly based on the law (1:7), it was full of Old Testament speculations ("myths and endless [wearisome] genealogies," 1:4); it was being presented as *gnōsis* ("knowledge," 6:20) and appeared to have an esoteric and exclusivistic appeal (1:4–7; note in 2:1–7 and 4:10 that God wants *all people* to be saved), which included a false asceticism that denied the goodness of creation (4:3–5; perhaps 5:23). Beyond their teaching, Paul indicts the teachers for their love of controversies, including battles over words (1:6; 6:4), and especially for their greed (6:5–10; cf. 3:3, "not a lover of money").

All in all, Paul has left Timothy with a very difficult assignment — which seems not to have been altogether successful in light of the evidence of 2 Timothy — making the words to Timothy all the more poignant. You might try to put yourself in Timothy's shoes as you read through the letter.

A WALK THROUGH I TIMOTHY

☐ 1:1–2   *Salutation*

Despite their long and close relationship, note how Paul emphasizes here his apostleship and Timothy's being his "true son" (= legitimate child). This is surely for the sake of the church, in light of what they must hear from this letter.

☐ 1:3–20   *First Charge to Timothy*

This first charge (v. 3, renewed in v. 18) reminds Timothy of his duty to stop the false teaching (v. 3), which is then described (vv. 4–11) in contrast to Paul's testimony (vv. 12–17). Notice how the latter both articulates the content of the gospel and authorizes Paul's apostleship. Verse 15 gives the first of three trustworthy sayings cited in this letter (see 3:1; 4:9) and emphasizes that Christ came to save sinners (not ascetics). The renewed charge (1:18–20) reminds the church that Hymenaeus and Alexander have been disfellowshipped.

☐ 2:1–15   *Instructions on Community Matters*

The first matter Paul brings up is community prayer, that it is to be for "everyone" (v. 1), because God wants "all people" to be saved (vv. 3–4), as Christ's sacrifice for "all people" is the sure evidence (vv. 5–6). This is followed by instruction about proper decorum at community prayer: When the men lift up their hands to pray, they are not to be soiled with the disputings of the false teachers (v. 8), and the women are not to dress seductively (for that culture), but to "wear" good deeds (vv. 9–10); because of the influence of the younger widows (2:15 and 5:14 should be read side by side), Paul forbids women to teach (using Eve's deception by Satan that led to transgression as the biblical analogy for their being deceived by Satan; cf. 4:1 and 5:15).

☐ 3:1–13   *Qualifications for Church Leaders*

With a second "trustworthy saying" (v. 1), Paul offers the character qualifications for three kinds of leaders (the verb "is to be" in v. 2 grammatically controls vv. 2, 8, and 12): overseers (vv. 1–7), deacons (vv. 8–10, 12), and women deacons ([v. 11], probably; certainly not "wives"). Note the singular lack of duties, except for "able to teach" in verse 2, and how many of these qualities stand in sharp contrast to what is said elsewhere of the false teachers.

☐ 3:14–4:5 *The Purpose for the Letter*

Paul writes so that God's people will know how to conduct themselves in God's household. They are to be God's temple (pillar and foundation) that preserves "the mystery from which true godliness springs," set forth in hymnic style in 3:16; this is set in direct contrast to the satanic teachings of the fallen elders (4:1–5). Note that the hymn emphasizes Christ's incarnation (line 1), apparently over against a false asceticism (4:3–5), and the universal nature of the gospel (lines 4–5), over against the (apparent) exclusivism of such asceticism.

☐ 4:6–16 *Renewed Charge to Timothy*

As in chapter 1, Timothy's charge is given over against the false teachers (vv. 6–8). The third trustworthy saying (v. 8) emphasizes that "training" in the godliness noted in 3:15–16 (versus ascetic "discipline") holds promise for life both in the present and the future, while the additional word about "labor" (= Paul's and Timothy's as ministers of the gospel) again emphasizes the universality of the gospel.

Notice how the rest of the charge (4:11–16), while clearly intended to bolster Timothy's courage, explicitly sets him before the congregation as a model to emulate—despite his youth—and reaffirms his ministry among them, before concluding with personal words.

☐ 5:1–6:2b *On Widows and Elders (and Slaves)*

Paul now specifies how to handle the two groups that have been causing the grief. After introductory words about all the people (5:1–2), he takes up in turn the younger widows (vv. 3–16) and the straying elders (vv. 17–25), concluding with instructions to slaves (6:1–2). Note how in both primary cases he first sets those who are going astray in contrast to those who are genuine. Thus the church is to care for "widows who are really in need" (5:3–9), but he counsels the younger ones to marry, bear children, and manage their households (vv. 11–16).

Likewise, the church must honor (and pay) faithful elders (5:17–18), but try (with impartiality), dismiss, and replace "those who sin" (vv. 19–22, 24–25). The parenthetical word to Timothy (v. 23) is probably for both his and the church's sake: "Keeping yourself pure" (v. 22) does not include (ascetic?) abstinence from wine, which Timothy needs for his health.

☐ 6:2c–10   *Final Indictment of the False Teachers*

Here Paul once more impeaches the false teachers for their love of controversy, but finally he scores them for their love of money. Note how he borrows here from the Old Testament Wisdom tradition (Job 1:21; Eccl 5:15).

☐ 6:11–20   *Final Charge to Timothy*

Note how, as in 4:1–16, Timothy is once again set in contrast to the false teachers, with emphasis now on his persevering to the end, "which God will bring about in his own time." Verses 17–19 qualify the indictment against greed in verses 6–10: Those who happen to be rich (in that culture, handed down as inheritance) are to be "rich in good deeds," especially in the form of generosity to the needy.

Note how the sign-off (vv. 20–21) summarizes Paul's urgencies; its abruptness highlights how urgent the matter is.

This letter's special contribution to the biblical story lies in its emphasizing the role of good leadership for the sake of the people of God, thus echoing the contrast between false and genuine prophets from the Old Testament.

2 Timothy

ORIENTING DATA FOR 2 TIMOTHY

- **Content:** an appeal to Timothy to remain loyal to Christ, to the gospel, and to Paul, including a final salvo at the false teachers (of 1 Timothy)

- **Author:** the apostle Paul (although doubted by many)

- **Date:** ca. A.D. 64, from a prison in Rome (the lion in 4:17 is an allusion to Nero or to the empire itself)

- **Recipient(s):** Timothy primarily; secondarily to the church (the first "you" in 4:22 is singular, the final one is plural)

- **Occasion:** Paul has been once more arrested and taken to Rome (most likely from Troas and at the instigation of Alexander, 4:13–15 [probably the same man who was disfellowshiped in 1 Tim 1:19–20]); the letter urges Timothy to come to Paul's side, but mostly offers him a kind of last will and testament

- **Emphases:** the saving work of Christ, "who has destroyed death and brought life ... through the gospel" (1:10); loyalty to Christ by perseverance in suffering and hardship; loyalty to Paul by recalling their longtime relationship; loyalty to the gospel by being faithful in proclaiming/teaching "the word" (= the gospel message); the deadly spread, but final demise, of the false teaching; the final salvation of those who are Christ's

OVERVIEW OF 2 TIMOTHY

This is Paul's final (preserved) letter. At the end, we learn that its primary purpose was to urge Timothy to join Paul in Rome posthaste (4:9, 21) and to bring Mark and some personal items along with him when he comes (4:11, 13). Timothy is to be replaced by Tychicus, the presumed bearer of the letter (4:12). The reason for haste is the onset of winter (4:21) and the fact that Paul's preliminary court hearing has already taken place (4:16).

But the majority of the letter is very little concerned about this matter and very much an appeal to Timothy to remain loyal to Paul and his gospel by embracing suffering and hardship. And in this sense it also becomes a community document (hence the plural "you" in 4:22b), implicitly urging the believers to loyalty as well. This appeal is made in the context of the continuing influence of the false teachers (2:16–18; 3:13), the defection of many (1:15), and Paul's expected execution (4:6–8).

Everything in the letter reflects these matters, including the thanksgiving (1:3–5) and the concluding personal matters and instructions (4:9–18). The body of the letter is comprised of three major appeals to loyalty (1:6–2:13; 2:14–3:9; 3:10–4:8), each of which follows a similar ABA pattern, which together create the same pattern for the whole letter. In the first appeal it is loyalty-defection-loyalty (1:6–14/1:15–18/2:1–13); in the second it is opposition-loyalty-opposition (2:14–19/2:20–26/3:1–9); in the third it is Paul's loyalty-appeal-Paul's loyalty (3:10–12/3:14–4:2, 5/4:6–8), interspersed with notes about opposition and desertion (3:13; 4:3–4). In the larger picture, the first and third sections are mostly appeal, while the sandwiched section is mostly about the opposition.

SPECIFIC ADVICE FOR READING 2 TIMOTHY

This letter does not fit comfortably the category Pastoral Epistle (see "Overview of 1 Timothy, pp. 373– 74), in the sense of offering instruction on church matters to a young pastor. But it is certainly pastoral in the sense of Paul's concern for Timothy personally, which is intertwined with his concern for Christ and the gospel. You may want to mark these instances as you read.

Second Timothy is not the first letter we have from Paul while he was "chained" (2:9). But in contrast to the earlier ones (Philippians, Colossians, Ephesians, Philemon), where he expects to be released (Phil 1:24; 2:23–24; Phlm 22), here he just as clearly expects to be executed (2 Tim 4:6–9, 16–18). Although this adds a dimension of poignancy to the whole (the desertions are obviously painful, 1:15; 4:9–12), there is no despair. To the contrary, hardship is simply part of the package (1:8; 2:3; 3:12; 4:5). You cannot miss the note of Christ's triumph over death and his bringing life, which rings out loud and clear (1:10; 2:8–10, 11–12a; 4:8, 18).

Even the long section condemning the false teachers (2:14–3:9) is interlaced with words of hope: "The Lord knows those who are his" (2:19, echoing Num 16:5). This section also helps to substantiate what you learned about the false teachers in 1 Timothy: They like to quarrel over words (2 Tim 2:14, 23); they have wandered away from the truth, arguing that the resurrection has already taken place (2:18); they have had noteworthy success among some "gullible women" (3:6–7); and their lifestyle does not conform to the gospel (3:1–5).

A WALK THROUGH 2 TIMOTHY

☐ 1:1–5 *Salutation and Thanksgiving*

Be on the lookout for the significance of the words in the salutation, "in keeping with the promise of life," for the rest of the letter. And note how, in contrast to 1 Timothy and Titus, which are more businesslike, this letter has a thanksgiving, which also (typically) anticipates much that is in the letter; note especially the emphasis on Paul's and Timothy's relationship, and on Timothy's loyalty to the faith of his forbears.

☐ 1:6–2:13 *First Appeal*

The first appeal sets the tone for the whole; it is basically two-fold—for Timothy to (1) join Paul in suffering for the gospel (v. 8) and (2) guard what has been entrusted to him (v. 13–14). The basis of the appeal is the work of the Spirit (vv. 6–7, 14), Christ and the gospel (vv. 9–10), and Paul's example (vv. 11–12).

The appeal is then interrupted to set in contrast the many who were not loyal (v. 15) and one who was (Onesiphorus, vv. 16–18).

Note the new twist when the appeal is renewed (2:1–13): Timothy must entrust to others what has been entrusted to him (v. 2)—because he is being pulled out of Ephesus. After a series of analogies emphasizing loyalty, single-mindedness, and expectation of final reward (vv. 3–7), Paul reinforces the appeal once more by reminding Timothy of Christ and of Paul himself (vv. 8–10), concluding with a "trustworthy saying" (vv. 11–13) that emphasizes God's faithfulness, no matter what.

☐ 2:14–3:9 *Context for the Appeal: The False Teachers*

You will want to notice that, as in 1 Timothy, words to Timothy are set in the context of the false teachers. The first warning against the false teachers (2 Tim 2:14–18) emphasizes their "quarreling about words" and "godless chatter" and their corrosive influence. Yet God "knows those who are his," and these "must turn away from wickedness" (v. 19, which prepares the way for what follows).

The contrasting appeal to Timothy (2:20–26) starts with an analogy (he must cleanse himself and the church of articles used for refuse) before emphasizing the need for a gentle, not quarrelsome, spirit—even in dealing with the opponents.

Paul returns to the false teachers in 3:1–9, describing their gruesome self-centeredness (vv. 1–5) and their deceitful sway over some "gullible women" (vv. 6–7), comparing them to the Egyptian sorcerers (vv. 8–9).

☐ 3:10–4:8 *Final Appeal*

The first appeal focused primarily on Christ and the gospel; this appeal focuses primarily on Timothy's long relationship to Paul, and Paul's own modeling of the gospel (3:10–13; 4:6–8). These two passages sandwich the appeal itself, first to Timothy's own past (3:14–17), and second to Timothy's ministry, given the many defections from the truth (4:1–5).

☐ 4:9–18 *The First Reason for the Letter*

Paul concludes with his primary reason for writing in the first place—to urge Timothy to come quickly (before winter, v. 21) and bring some personal things with him (vv. 9, 13). This is said against the backdrop of deserters and some others having been sent out on ministry (vv. 10–12). Since Timothy will come through Troas, Paul warns him about Alexander (vv. 14–15). He concludes with information about his "first defense" (= a kind of grand-jury inquiry), which for him was a moment of triumph for the gospel. Rescued from the "lion's mouth" in this first instance, he nonetheless looks forward to the heavenly kingdom.

☐ 4:19–22 *Final Greetings*

Unlike 1 Timothy, 2 Timothy is more truly a letter in its overall style; thus it concludes with greetings to and from friends, plus the grace-benediction.

With this letter Paul's role in the biblical story comes to an end. Since we are so much in his debt, we would do well to heed carefully the appeals to loyalty in this letter.

Titus

ORIENTING DATA FOR TITUS

- **Content:** instructions to Titus for setting in order the church(es) on Crete, including the appointment of qualified elders and the instruction of various social groups, set against the backdrop of some false teachers

- **Author:** the apostle Paul (although doubted by many)

- **Date:** ca. A.D. 62–63, apparently from Macedonia at about the same time as 1 Timothy (see 3:12; Nicopolis is on the Adriatic coast of Macedonia)

- **Recipient(s):** Titus, a Gentile and sometime traveling companion of Paul (see Gal 2:1–3; 2 Cor 7:6–16; 8:6, 16–24; 12:17–18); and the churches on Crete (Titus 3:15, "you all")

- **Occasion:** Paul had left Titus on Crete to finish setting the churches in order, while he and Timothy (apparently) went on to Ephesus, where they met a very distressing situation (see 1 Timothy). But Paul had to go on to Macedonia (1 Tim 1:3; cf. Phil 2:19–24); perhaps the Holy Spirit reminded him while writing 1 Timothy that some similar problems had emerged in Crete, so he addressed the churches through a letter to Titus

- **Emphases:** God's people must be and do good—this is especially true of church leaders; the gospel of grace stands over against false teachings based on the Jewish law

OVERVIEW OF TITUS

In some ways Titus appears to be a smaller version of 1 Timothy, where false teaching prompted instruction on qualifications for church leadership; at the same time Paul addresses other matters that the false teachers have triggered. Hence, both the qualifications for elders and

137

the indictment of the false teachers have some striking similarities to what is said about them in 1 Timothy.

But there are also some significant differences. The most noteworthy is the fact that *Timothy* was left in a situation where the church had been in existence for nearly twelve years, and he had to deal with elders who were leading the church astray. *Titus* has been left in Crete to set new churches in order. Thus, in this case, Paul begins with the qualifications for church leaders (1:5–9), before taking on the false teachers (1:10–16). This is followed by general instructions on how to deal with older and younger men and women and with slaves, with emphasis on doing good (2:1–10), which looks like an expansion of 1 Timothy 5:1–2 and 6:1–2. The rest of the letter then emphasizes, in light of the grace of God, their "doing good" in the world (2:11–3:8), which is again set in contrast to the false teachers (3:9–11).

SPECIFIC ADVICE FOR READING TITUS

While problems with the false teachers lie behind much of what is said in Titus, they do not seem to be such a dominant factor as in 1 Timothy. They themselves are to be silenced (Titus 1:11), while people who would follow them must be rebuked (1:13). There are enough similarities with 1 Timothy to make one think that the same kind of teaching is in view: They are into Jewish myths (Titus 1:14) and genealogies (3:9), based on the law (3:9); they love controversies (1:10; 3:9); they are deceivers (1:10) and lovers of money (1:11); and they use the law (apparently) to promote ascetic practices (1:15). This final item gets more emphasis in Titus, which Paul responds to with a much greater emphasis both on grace and on doing good.

So as you read, look especially for Paul's emphasis on *doing good*. Although found also in 1 Timothy (1 Tim 2:10; 5:10), this theme permeates Titus (Titus 1:16; 2:7, 14; 3:1, 8, 14; cf. 1:8). For Paul there is no tension between grace and doing what is good. The latter is the proper issue of the former. What is at odds with grace is the "religious" use of the law, maintaining purity through observance of regulations, as a way of maintaining God's favor. But a genuine experience of grace results in a people who are eager to do good (2:14). Thus these two themes merge in two great theological passages (2:11–14; 3:4–7), the latter of which constitutes another of the five trustworthy sayings in these letters.

A WALK THROUGH TITUS

☐ **1:1–4** *Salutation*

As with 1 Timothy, and in contrast to 2 Timothy, this letter is more "business" than personal, thus it lacks a thanksgiving/prayer report. For whose sake (Titus's or the churches'), do you think, is the long elaboration on Paul's apostleship? After you've read through the whole letter, you might want to come back to this passage and list the ways it anticipates items in the letter.

☐ **1:5–9** *Appointing Elders*

This list is very similar to 1 Timothy 3:2–7. The fact that "appointment" is in view here (not "replacement") is expressly stated (Titus 1:5), which also accounts for the one major difference with 1 Timothy, namely, the *duties* mentioned in Titus 1:9. On their being "hospitable" (v. 8), see 3 John. And don't miss the next item in Titus 1:8: They are to "love what is good."

☐ **1:10–16** *Opposing False Teachers*

The false teachers must be silenced because they play right into the hands of a proverbial understanding of Cretans. Believers who would be tempted to follow them must be rebuked. Again note how the section ends: These people are "unfit for doing anything good."

☐ **2:1–10** *Godly Living for Various Social Groups*

Picking up the same four groups as in 1 Timothy 5:1–2, plus the slaves from 6:1–2, Paul gives instructions on "sound doctrine." (medical imagery for being healthy) for older men, older women, younger women, younger men, and slaves. Note how often the reasons given for godly living are for the sake of those on the outside (Titus 2:5, 8, 10). Again, note verse 7: Titus is to set an example "by doing what is good."

☐ **2:11–15** *The Basis for Godly Living*

Now Titus is given the theological bases for the preceding instructions—the grace of God, our future hope, and Christ's redemption, which has as its goal a people of his own, who are "eager to do what is good" (v. 14).

☐ 3:1–8 *The People of God in the World*

As in 2:1–10, notice how "doing good" is pointed outward—how to live in a godly manner for the sake of an ungodly world (3:1–2), since we were once there ourselves (v. 3). The basis for such living is salvation wrought by the Triune God (vv. 4–7)—rebirth initiated by God's love and effected through Christ's justifying grace and the renewing work of the Holy Spirit, who is poured out on us generously through Christ. Verse 8 offers the motive.

☐ 3:9–11 *Final Indictment of the False Teachers*

You might want to compare what is said here with 1:10–16. Thus the letter signs off the way it began.

☐ 3:12–15 *Concluding Personal Notes and Greetings*

Note that after some personal words to Titus about his and others' comings and goings (vv. 12–13), Paul hits the main theme of "doing what is good" one final time (v. 14), before a concluding exchange of greetings and the grace-benediction.

The significance of this letter for the biblical story is Paul's insistence that grace and doing good belong together, as long as the latter is not confused with religious observances.

Philemon

ORIENTING DATA FOR PHILEMON

- **Content:** the sole purpose of this letter is to secure forgiveness for a (probably runaway) slave named Onesimus

- **Author:** the apostle Paul, joined by his younger companion Timothy

- **Date:** probably A.D. 60–61 (see "Orienting Data for Colossians," p. 359).

- **Recipient(s):** Philemon is a Gentile believer in Colosse (see Col 4:9), in whose house a church meets; the salutation and final greeting indicate that Paul expected Philemon to share the letter with the church

- **Occasion:** Onesimus has recently been converted and has been serving Paul, who is in prison; now Onesimus is being sent back to Philemon, accompanied by Tychicus, who is also carrying letters to the churches in Colosse (Colossians) and Asia (Ephesians)

- **Emphasis:** the gospel reconciles people to one another, not only Jew (Paul) and Gentile (Philemon), but also (runaway) slave and master, making them all brothers!

OVERVIEW OF PHILEMON

This, the shortest of Paul's letters, was an extremely delicate letter to write. Paul is explicitly asking forgiveness for a crime that deserved punishment (Onesimus's crime) — and implicitly for another crime that could have been brought before the proper authorities (Paul's harboring a runaway slave).

You will want to observe how carefully Paul puts all of this into gospel perspective, beginning with the prayer and thanksgiving (vv. 4–7), where he praises God for the way the gospel has already been at work in Philemon's life. Note especially that Paul refuses to lean on his apostolic authority (see vv. 1, 8–10, 17, 21); rather, he appeals on the basis of the gospel of love (vv. 8–11). He also reminds Philemon that he, too, is one of Paul's converts (v. 19), whom he regards now as a "partner" in the gospel (v. 17).

Verses 12–16 are the coup. Onesimus has really been in the service of Philemon without his knowing it, and his having been a runaway may finally serve the greater interests of all, especially the gospel. Even though Onesimus is returning as a repentant slave, the first relationship between slave and master, Paul reminds Philemon, is that of brother in Christ.

SPECIFIC ADVICE FOR READING PHILEMON

Slavery in the first-century Greco-Roman world was not based on capture and race, as in North American (and European) history, but, by Paul's time, on economics—and birth. But even household slaves, as Onesimus probably was, were at the bottom of the social ladder, having absolutely no rights under Roman law. Thus they could be treated as a master willed, and runaways were often crucified as a deterrent to other slaves.

So imagine yourself in Onesimus's shoes. Apparently he had stolen from Philemon (vv. 18–19) and run away as far as he could get (Rome). But he became repentant, fell in with Paul, who was in prison in Rome, and now, back home, stands in the midst of the Christian community, while Colossians and this letter are read to the congregation. How do you think you would feel?

But we may surmise that the letter had already been read by Philemon so that the reading of it in church was a public expression of Philemon's acceptance of both Paul's letter and his wishes. You might also want to go back and do a quick reread of Colossians, keeping in mind that the Colossian believers are hearing it read with Onesimus present and that they, too, must accept Onesimus back as "a dear brother" in Christ.

Did the letter work? Of course it did; it is hard to imagine either of these letters being preserved if it hadn't! Whether this Onesimus is the one who eventually became overseer of the church in Ephesus cannot be known for certain, but Christian tradition believed it so. We know about him from Ignatius, who, on his way to Rome to be martyred, wrote to the church in Ephesus: "In God's name, therefore, I received your large congregation in the person of Onesimus, your bishop in this world, a man whose love is beyond words. My prayer is that you should love him in the

Spirit of Jesus Christ and all be like him. Blessed is he who let you have such a bishop. You deserved it." The gospel does things like that!

A WALK THROUGH PHILEMON

☐ 1–3 *Salutation*

Fortunately, the salutation proper gives us a lot of helpful information noted under "Orienting Data for Philemon." (Apphia is probably Philemon's wife; in light of Col 4:17, Archippus is likely a teacher in the church). In any case, be certain that Onesimus's return will affect the whole household, as well as the church.

☐ 4–7 *Thanksgiving and Prayer*

As in Paul's other thanksgiving and prayer reports, he thanks God and prays mostly for the effects of the gospel in Philemon's life. Note the emphasis on love and faith (v. 5), which are then elaborated in reverse order in verses 6 and 7; note also how the end of verse 7 anticipates what is coming.

☐ 8–21 *The Appeal*

Watch for the wordplay on Onesimus's name in verses 10–11. The formerly-useless-now-useful one is urged not only to be welcomed (v. 17), but taken back as a "brother in the Lord." It is not clear how Paul could have repaid Onesimus's debt (vv. 18–19)—after all, Paul is in prison and wholly dependent on outside help himself! He surely expects Philemon to wipe the slate clean, but just in case, he models the gospel by taking on the debt himself.

☐ 22–25 *Personal Word and Greetings*

Verse 22 indicates that Paul expects release from this imprisonment (cf. Phil 1:24; 2:23–24), a concern that in this case takes the place of "greet all the saints," which usually occurs. You may wish to compare the greetings in Philemon 23–24 with those in Colossians 4:10–15.

This semiprivate letter is in our Bibles because the truth of the gospel lies not only in its history and the theological interpretation of that history; it is also anecdotal. God's story has been told a million times over in stories like this one.

Hebrews

ORIENTING DATA FOR HEBREWS

■ **Content:** a "word of exhortation" (13:22) sent in letter form, encouraging faithful perseverance in light of the superlative final word God has spoken in Christ

■ **Author:** unknown; a second-generation believer (2:3), who was a skilled preacher and interpreter of Scripture, with an excellent command of Greek (it came into the canon among Paul's letters, but definitely not by him)

■ **Date:** unknown; guesses range from A.D. 50 to 90; probably before 70 (since the author gives no hint that the Jewish temple has been destroyed)

■ **Recipients:** an unknown but specific group of (predominantly) Jewish Christians; perhaps a house church in Rome (13:24) that is opting out of relationships with the larger Christian community (10:25; 13:7, 17)

■ **Occasion:** the community is discouraged because of suffering (10:35–39) and perhaps from doubts about whether Jesus really took care of sin; the author writes to convince them to "not throw away your confidence" (10:35; cf. 2:1; 4:14)

■ **Emphases:** God has spoken his absolutely final word in his Son; to abandon Christ is to abandon God altogether; Christ is superior to everything that went before—the old revelation, its angelic mediators, the first exodus (Moses and Joshua), and the whole priestly system; God's people can have full confidence in God's Son, the perfect high priest, who gives all people ready access to God

OVERVIEW OF HEBREWS

Hebrews is a long, sustained argument, in which the author moves back and forth between an argument (based on Scripture) and exhortation. What drives the argument from beginning to end is the absolute superiority of the Son of God to everything that has gone before; this is what his *exposition of Scripture* is all about. What concerns the author is the possibility that some believers under present distress will let go of Christ and thus lose out on the Son's saving work and high priestly intercession, and thus their own experience of God's presence; this is what the interspersed *exhortations* are all about.

The introduction (1:1–3) sets the pattern with a sevenfold description of the Son and his work that makes him God's last word. This is followed by a series of two major arguments (1:4–4:13; 4:14–10:18), each with several subsets, and a final major application and exhortation (10:19–13:21), in this case interlaced with some further biblical arguments.

Part 1 is all about the Son—his superiority to angels despite (and because of!) his humanity (1:4–2:18), to Moses (3:1–19), and to Joshua (4:1–13). Here the author also sets the stage for part 2: Christ's effective high priestly ministry is made possible through the preexistent and now exalted Son's having become incarnate. And the failure of the first exodus lay not with Moses and Joshua, but with the people's failure to faithfully persevere; the readers are urged not to follow in their footsteps.

Part 2 is all about the Son as the perfect high priest. After a transitional exhortation (4:14–16), the author then introduces Jesus as high priest (5:1–10), followed by a series of two warnings and an encouragement (5:11–6:3 [slacking off]; 6:4–8 [apostasy]; 6:9–20 [God's sure promises]). Then, drawing on the royal messianic Psalm 110, he uses Melchizedek as a pattern for a priesthood of a higher order (7:1–28). Based on a new, thus superior, covenant, the perfect priest offered the perfect (once-for-all) sacrifice in the perfect sanctuary (8:1–10:18).

Part 3 is all about faithful perseverance. It begins with an appeal—in light of all this, "let us ..." (10:19–25)—followed by warning (10:26–31), encouragement (10:32–39), example (11:1–12:3), instruction (12:4–13), and another warning (12:14–17). Finally, using marvelous imagery that contrasts Mount Sinai with the heavenly Mount Zion, the author affirms their future certainty (12:18–29), then concludes with very practical exhortations about life in the present (13:1–25).

You will want to watch how the author makes this work—by a series of seven expositions of key Old Testament texts, while making the transition between each by way of exhortation: (1) Psalm 8:4–6 in Hebrews 2:5–18; (2) Psalm 95:7–11 in 3:7–4:13; (3) Psalm 110:4 in 4:16–7:28; (4) Jeremiah 31:31–34 in 8:1–10:18; (5) Habakkuk 2:3–4 in 10:32–12:3; (6) Proverbs 3:11–12 in 12:4–13; and (7) the Sinai theophany (Exod 19) in 12:18–29.

SPECIFIC ADVICE FOR READING HEBREWS

Most contemporary Christians do not find Hebrews an easy read, for at least two reasons: (1) its structure (just noted) of a single, sustained argument, interlaced with application and exhortations, and (2) the author's thought-world (basic ways of perceiving reality), which is so foreign to ours. Thus there are two keys to a good reading.

First, keep in sight the two foci that concern the author throughout: (1) the overwhelming majesty of Jesus, the Son of God, who stands at the beginning and the end of all things and whose suffering in his incarnation made him a perfect high priest on their behalf (he both dealt with sin finally and perfectly and is also a merciful and empathetic intercessor), and (2) all of this is spoken into the present despondency of the people to whom he writes, who have had a long siege of hardship (10:32–39) and who are beginning to wonder whether Jesus really is God's final answer. Try to put yourself in their shoes: Jews who had long ago put their trust in Christ, believing that at long last the fulfillment of their messianic hopes had come—only to have suffering (and sin) continue long after they had first believed.

Second, since everything for him (and them) hinges on his exposition of Scripture as pointing to Christ, it is especially important for you to have a sense of how the writer of Hebrews uses Scripture and what Scriptures he actually uses.

Four things are important about his use of Scripture: (1) His and their only Bible was the Septuagint, the Greek translation of the Hebrew Bible. This means at times that his citations, which are very exact, do not always read as does your Old Testament, and sometimes his point is made from the wording in the Greek Bible. (2) He regularly uses a very common rabbinic way of arguing, namely, "from the lesser to the greater" (= if something is true of *a*, how much more so of *z*). (3) He reads the entire Old Testament through the lens of Christ, understanding well that the royal psalms point to David's greater son, the Messiah. (4) His form of scriptural argument is to cite his text and then show how other texts and the event of Christ support his reading of these texts.

It is especially important for you to be aware of what Scripture the author actually cites and then argues from. For example, even though he alludes to the sacrificial system in 9:1–10:18, he never cites from Leviticus. Rather, he focuses his argument almost altogether on Jesus as fulfilling a key royal psalm—Psalm 110. At the same time he presupposes that Jesus also fulfills the first royal psalm—Psalm 2. The latter declares that the Messiah is God's Son (Ps 2:7), which is the very *first* thing the author says in his introduction (Heb 1:2). He then elaborates in terms of the Son's being heir (as well as the Creator and Sustainer) of the universe, and of his being "the radiance of God's glory and the exact representation of his being." Psalm 2:7, joined with the Davidic covenant (2 Sam 7:14), is then the first citation (Heb 1:5) in the series of proof texts that follow. You will find it cited again—for the final time—in 5:5, where it is joined with a citation from Psalm 110:4.

Observe next how the *last* thing said in the introduction of the Son (Heb 1:1–3) is that he "provided purification for sins" and "sat down at the right hand of the Majesty in heaven." These allusions to Psalm 110 (vv. 4, 1) are then picked up as the final citation in the following series (Heb 1:13). Thus in this one messianic psalm, you find two crucial matters: (1) the Son, now called "Lord," is seated at the right hand of God (Ps 110:1), the place of his high priestly ministry (see Heb 8:1; 10:12; 12:2), and (2) God by oath promised that the exalted King/Son will also be a priest forever in the order of Melchizedek (Ps 110:4). So after the author joins Psalm 110:4 to Psalm 2:7 in 5:5–6, the rest of the argument from that point on will be about Christ's fulfilling this promise.

Now add to these points the following: (1) the failure of Israel to enter into rest (Heb 3–4, based on Ps 95); (2) the fact that God promised a new covenant (Jer 31:31–34, cited in full in Heb 8:8–12); (3) the fact that Christ's death effected both that new covenant and a perfect, once-for-all sacrifice for sins (9:1–10:18, thus bringing the old order to an end); (4) the long list (ch. 11) of those who faithfully persevered as they awaited the future promise; and (5) the concluding analogy in 12:18–29 of the superiority of heavenly Zion to Mount Sinai—and you should be able to see not only where the whole argument is going but also how persuasive it should have been for these early Jewish Christians. So read and enjoy!

A WALK THROUGH HEBREWS

☐ **1:1–3** *Introduction*

Watch how these verses offer a true introduction to the argument: The Son, who is superior to the prophets, is the heir of all things; he also stands at the beginning of all things. Moreover, he who is God's glory, being his exact representation, also presently sustains all things; and it is he who dealt with sin and now sits at the place of authority at God's right hand.

☐ **1:4–4:13** *The Supremacy of God's Son*

Here you enter at once into the author's way of arguing, as he begins with a series of Old Testament quotations (1:4–14) that do two things simultaneously—show the Son's superiority to angels and support the affirmations of verses 2–3.

After an initial warning (2:1–4), he expounds Psalm 8:4–6 to argue for the significance of the Incarnation: The Son was made "lower than the angels" for a brief time so that he could (1) fully identity with us, (2) through his sufferings effect salvation for us, and (3) thus also become a merciful high priest for us—and therefore be better than the angels.

Next you come to the author's contrast with Moses (Heb 3:1–6; note the form of argument, from the lesser to the greater). The mention of Christ's superiority to Moses leads to exhortation and warning, based on Psalm 95:7–11, that those who are Christ's must not follow in the unbelief (= lack of faithful obedience) of those who belonged to Moses (Heb 3:7–19). Watch how this in turn leads to a further exposition on the theme of entering God's rest (4:1–10; from Ps 95:11), which the first Joshua ("Jesus" in Greek) did not secure, and which now awaits those who persevere. The transitional exhortation (Heb 4:11–13) serves to remind the Jewish Christians of the certainty of God's word.

☐ **4:14–10:18** *The Supremacy of the Son's High Priesthood*

In this section you will encounter the author's long, sustained argument about Jesus as the ultimate high priest. The theme is introduced by way of a transitional exhortation (4:14–16), which picks up the theme from 2:17–3:1 and urges that Christ as high priest makes it possible for all people, not just priests, to "approach God's throne of grace with confidence, so that we may receive mercy"—because Christ also shared our humanity, with all of its suffering.

The sustained argument then begins in 5:1–10 with an exposition of Psalm 110:1 and 4, emphasizing first the humanity and duties of priests and their divine appointment, before citing the two royal psalms and showing how Jesus' humanity and suffering qualified him for priestly service—but now of a new and higher order, namely, that of Melchizedek.

Before the author elaborates this point, he feels constrained to remonstrate with them over their slowness to become mature (Heb 5:11–6:3), which leads to a warning against apostasy (6:4–8), but note that he concludes with encouragement (6:9–12). As he begins to move back to the exposition about Melchizedek, he argues that God's promise (Ps 110:4, about the Messiah's priesthood) is confirmed by his oath in the same verse, thus making his promise absolutely guaranteed (Heb 6:13–20).

The exposition about Melchizedek is in two parts: First (7:1–10), the author draws on the Genesis account (Gen 14:18–20) and glories in Melchizedek's lack of a genealogy (no predecessor or human successor) and in the fact that Levi (understood to be present in Abraham's loins) is already foreshadowed as inferior to the greater; second (Heb 7:11–28), the author shows that, by fitting the Melchizedek order, Christ's priesthood is both legitimate and superior to that of Aaron.

Not only so, but (8:1–6) Christ's priesthood takes place in a superior sanctuary (heaven itself; note the allusion to Ps 110:1 in Heb 8:1) and is based on the new (and thus superior) covenant promised in Jeremiah (Heb 8:7–13). Watch how the exposition that follows shows how Christ, the perfect "sacrificer," is also the superior (perfect) sacrifice (9:1–10:18). After describing the old (9:1–10), he shows how Christ's sacrifice of himself both obtained eternal redemption (9:11–14) and mediated the new covenant through his death (9:15–22). He then summarizes the argument and brings it to a conclusion (9:23–10:18) by emphasizing the eternal, "once for all time" nature of Christ's sacrifice (no condemnation for past or present sins!).

☐ **10:19–12:29** *Final Exhortation to Perseverance*

Note how the author's concerns emerge in the five "let us" exhortations in 10:22–25, based on the sure work of Christ (vv. 19–21): Let us draw near to God (we now have access to the Most Holy Place!); let us hold fast to our hope; let us spur one another on toward love and good deeds; let us not forsake meeting together with others; and let us encourage one another. After a strong warning against deliberate sin (grace does not mean license; vv. 26 – 31), he urges perseverance (vv. 32 – 39), citing Habakkuk 2:3 – 4.

The exposition of the Habakkuk text that follows (Heb 11:1 – 12:3) is so well known that it is easy to miss what is going on. Note that the author's singular point is the faith (faithful perseverance) of many who did not "shrink back" (10:39) — despite adversity and not obtaining the promised future; at the same time he insists that we are in continuity with these believers and they with us, since the promise has now been realized as we all await the glorious future. He concludes by pointing his readers once more to Jesus as an example of endurance in suffering (12:1 – 3).

Besides, he goes on (with an exposition of Prov 3:11 – 12), there is an educative dimension to suffering. After a final exhortation to holy living in community (Heb 12:14 – 17), he concludes with the analogy of the two mountains (12:18 – 24), including both warning and encouragement (12:25 – 29).

□ **13:1 – 25** *Concluding Practical Exhortations and Greetings*

Watch for the ways these exhortations emphasize his readers' need to love others in the community and to submit to their leaders, all the while still contrasting Christ with what has preceded him (thus, e.g., the sacrificial system is out, but a sacrifice of praise and of doing good to others is in [vv. 15 – 16]).

This is an especially important document in the biblical story in that it shows both the continuity of the new with the old (Christ has fulfilled the old, thus completing its purpose) and the nature of discontinuity (the people of God are now newly constituted through God's royal Son and the Spirit) — all of this by the one and only living God.

James

ORIENTING DATA FOR JAMES

- **Content:** a treatise composed of short moral essays, emphasizing endurance in hardship and responsible Christian living, with special concern that believers practice what they preach and live together in harmony

- **Author:** James, brother of our Lord (Gal 1:19), who led the church in Jerusalem for many years (Acts 15; Gal 2:1–13)—although questioned by many

- **Date:** unknown; dated anywhere from the mid–40s A.D. to the 90s, depending on authorship; probably earlier than later

- **Recipients:** believers in Christ among the Jewish Diaspora

- **Occasion:** unknown, but the treatise shows concern for real conditions in the churches, including severe trials, dissensions caused by angry and judgmental words, and abuse of the poor by the wealthy

- **Emphases:** practical faith on the part of believers; joy and patience in the midst of trials; the nature of true (Christian) wisdom; attitudes of the rich toward the poor; abuse and proper use of the tongue

OVERVIEW OF JAMES

Traditionally James has been read as a more or less random collection of ethical instructions for believers in general. But there is probably more order to it than first meets the eye. The main concerns are mapped out in 1:2–18, which basically takes the form of consolation to believers in exile: Trials may serve to test for the good (vv. 2–4, 12) or tempt toward evil (vv. 13–15); wisdom is God's good gift for enduring and profiting from trials (vv. 5–8, 16–18); in God's eyes the low and high position of poor and rich are reversed (vv. 9–11).

The next section (1:19–2:26) is in three parts, held together by James's concern that his hearers put their faith into practice—at the very practical level of one's speech and of caring for the poor. He begins by denouncing community dissension, insisting that people actually do what the word says, not just talk about it (1:19–25). This is applied specifically to the tongue and to caring for the poor (vv. 26–27) and then to wrong attitudes toward the rich and the poor (2:1–13). He concludes the section where he began, by insisting that faith must be accompanied by deeds appropriate to faith (vv. 14–26).

The next section (3:1–4:12) returns to the matter of dissension within the believing communities. He starts with the perennial problem child—the tongue (3:1–12; cf. 1:26), which in this case is aimed at their teachers in particular. Returning to the theme of true wisdom, which leads to peace (3:13–18; cf. 1:5–8), James then attacks their quarrels head-on (4:1–12).

Related to the way that the first mention of wisdom (1:5–8) is followed by a blessing of the poor and warnings to the rich, here in reverse order there is a twofold word to the rich (4:13–17; 5:1–6) and a call to patience on the part of the suffering poor (5:7–11). The letter concludes with a warning against oaths (v. 12), a call to prayer—especially prayer for the sick (vv. 13–18)—and correction of the wayward (vv. 19–20).

SPECIFIC ADVICE FOR READING JAMES

James is admittedly difficult to read through, because of its many starts and stops, twists and turns. But along with seeing the threads that hold things together, which we noted above, several other matters should help you to read this letter with better understanding.

First, in terms of content, you will find the letter to have a variety of kinds of material in it, all of it directed specifically at Christian behavior, rather than propounding Christian doctrine. Included are a goodly number of sayings or aphorisms that look like Old Testament wisdom on the one hand and the teachings of Jesus on the other. That is, much as the Synoptic Gospels often present the teaching of Jesus in the form of sayings—which at times ring with echoes of Jewish wisdom—so with James. This is found both in his emphasis on wisdom as such and in the frequent aphoristic nature of so much that he says. In this vein you should also look for his frequent echoes of the teachings of Jesus (e.g., 1:5–6; 2:8; 5:9, 12). As with all Jewish wisdom (see the introduction to the Old Testament Writings, p. 120), the concern is not doctrinal or logical, but practical; the test of its truthfulness has to do with how it works out in the reality of everyday life.

Second, in terms of form, you will find a kind of sermonic quality to James. As you read, note the various rhetorical devices he employs, especially some that reflect the Greco-Roman diatribe (see "Specific Advice for Reading Romans," p. 319)—direct address ("my [dear] brothers and sisters" 14x), rhetorical questions (e.g., Jas 2:3–7, 14, 21; 3:11–12, 13; 4:1, 5), and the use of an imagined interlocutor (2:18–20; 4:12, 13, 15). Thus James's use of the Wisdom tradition is not proverbial but sermonic; he hopes to persuade and thus to facilitate change in the way God's people live in community with one another.

Third, don't fall into the habit, which is easy in this case, of reading James as though it were addressed to individual believers about their one-on-one relationship with God and others. Nothing could be further from James's own concerns. From the outset his passion is with life within the believing community. While it is true that each must assume his or her individual responsibility to make the community healthy, the concern is not with personal piety as much as it is with healthy communities. To miss this point will cause you to miss what drives this letter from beginning to end.

Finally, you need to read the sections about the rich and poor with care (1:9–11, 27; 2:1–13; 4:13–5:6), since it is not easy to tell whether both groups are members of the believing community. In any case, James is decidedly—as is the whole of Scripture—on the side of the poor. The rich are consistently censured and judged, not because of their wealth per se, but because it has caused them to live without taking God into account and thus to abuse the lowly ones for whom God cares.

A WALK THROUGH JAMES

☐ **1:1–18** *Salutation and Introduction to the Themes*

Here James introduces most of his major concerns. Note how, after a letter-type salutation (v. 1), he jumps immediately into the issue of trials, urging joy because trials develop perseverance and lead to maturity (vv. 2–4; anticipating 5:7–11). Next he urges prayer for wisdom (1:5; anticipating 3:13–18), insisting that prayer must be accompanied by faith to be effective (1:6–8; anticipating 5:13–18). That leads to the major concern about the poor and rich, offering hope to the former and warning the latter (1:9–11; anticipating 1:27–2:13; 4:13–5:6); here note the echoes of Isaiah 40:6–8, which is also expressed in a context of comfort for exiles. Returning to the matter of trials and testing, he notes that they can lead beyond testing to *temptation* (only one Greek word for both ideas), for which God is not to be blamed (Jas 1:12–15), concluding that God instead gives only good gifts, especially "birth through the word of truth" (vv. 16–18).

☐ 1:19–2:26   *Putting the Faith into Practice*

As you read this section, think about what gives it a measure of cohesion. Starting with anger and the tongue, James moves next to urge that his readers live out the word they hear, especially regarding the tongue and caring for the poor (1:19–27). To care for the poor means to show no favoritism toward the rich; to do so is sin, and to do otherwise—to lack mercy—means to come under judgment (2:1–13). Finally, he attacks those who understand faith as mere verbal assent to doctrines believed; to speak about faith without tangibly caring for the poor—that is, faith without action—is to be dead (vv. 14–26).

☐ 3:1–4:12   *Dissension in the Community*

You may wish to go back and reread 1:19–27 before you read this section. Here James turns to the large issue of dissension in the believing communities, beginning with what has become the classic exposition of the use and abuse of the tongue (3:1–12); the tongue is "a restless evil, full of deadly poison" (v. 8). Can you relate? Similar to the preceding admonition against "faith without deeds," here he is concerned about the same tongue being used to praise God and curse others.

This in turn leads directly to a return to the theme of wisdom (3:13–18), contrasting godly wisdom with what is false and insisting on true wisdom as being pure and peace-loving.

Note that these two matters (the tongue and wisdom) together serve to introduce the crucial issue of quarreling within the believing community (4:1–12). In turn, James exposes its sinful roots (vv. 1–3), its worldliness (vv. 4–5), and the need for humility (vv. 6–10), returning at the end to the abuse of the tongue in judging one another (vv. 11–12).

☐ 4:13–5:11   *To the Rich and the Poor*

Note that this is the third time James takes up the issue of the rich and the poor, suggesting that it is a major concern. Although we cannot be sure, he seems to speak first to wealthy believers, who treat their business in a worldly fashion (4:13–17). This is followed by a harsh denunciation of wealthy farmers (apparently unbelievers), who abuse their workers by underpaying them (5:1–6).

Finally, returning to the issue of trials, probably in this case to the suffering poor, he once more urges perseverance (vv. 7–11; cf. 1:3).

☐ 5:12–20   *Concluding Exhortations*

The concluding exhortations seem somewhat more loosely connected to what has preceded. He begins with oaths (v. 12), clearly echoing the teaching of Jesus (Matt 5:33–37); he then turns to prayer and faith (Jas 5:13–18; cf. 1:6–8), especially showing concern for the poor (the "sick" in this case). He concludes with a blessing on those who restore the wanderer (5:19–20). Note the lack of any letter-type conclusion.

James is the New Testament counterpart of the Jewish Wisdom tradition, now in light of the teachings of Jesus. Although James is sometimes read in contrast to Paul, both James and Paul are, in fact, absolutely together at the crucial point made by James throughout his letter, namely, that the first thing one does with one's faith is to live by it (cf. Gal 5:6).

1 Peter

ORIENTING DATA FOR 1 PETER

- **Content:** a letter of encouragement to Christians undergoing suffering, instructing them how to respond Christianly to their persecutors and urging them to live lives worthy of their calling

- **Author:** the apostle Peter; written by Silas (5:12), the sometime companion of Paul

- **Date:** ca. A.D. 64–65 from Rome (5:13, Babylon was used by both Jews and Christians to refer to Rome as a place of exile)

- **Recipients:** mostly Gentile believers (1:14, 18; 2:9–10; 4:3–4) in the five provinces in the northwest quadrant of Asia Minor (modern Turkey), referred to — with a play on the Jewish Diaspora — as strangers (= exiles) in the world

- **Occasion:** probably concern over an outbreak of local persecution that some newer believers (2:2–3) were experiencing as a direct result of their faith in Christ

- **Emphases:** suffering for the sake of righteousness should not surprise us; believers should submit to unjust suffering the way Christ did; Christ suffered on our behalf to free us from sin; God's people should live righteously at all times, but especially in the face of hostility; our hope for the future is based on the certainty of Christ's resurrection

OVERVIEW OF 1 PETER

Peter's primary concern is for truly Christian living in the context of hostility and suffering. The letter moves forward in a kind of elliptical way, embracing first one and then the other of these concerns, returning to them over and over again along the way. At the same time these concerns are placed within the context of Christ's suffering and resurrection, his suffering offering a pattern for believers as well as saving them, his resurrection giving them hope in the midst of present suffering.

The opening thanksgiving (1:3–12) sets forth the themes: salvation, hope for the future, suffering, genuine faith (= faithful living). The rest of the letter falls into three parts (1:13–2:10; 2:11–4:11; 4:12–5:11), signaled by the address "dear friends" in 2:11 and 4:12 (and the doxology in 4:11). Part 1 is a call to holy living, with emphasis on their life together as the people of God. Using all kinds of images from the Old Testament, Peter reassures them that they are God's people by election, whose lives together are to give evidence that they are God's children and thus declare God's praises.

Part 2 focuses primarily on their being God's people for the sake of the pagan world (2:12)—those responsible for their suffering. He begins (2:11–3:7) by urging Christlike submission in specific institutional settings (pagan government [2:13–17]; pagan masters [2:18–25]; pagan husbands [3:1–6]) in which believers may expect to suffer. He then generalizes this appeal to all believers (3:8–4:6), specifically when facing suffering for doing good; again, Christ's death and resurrection serve as the basis for holiness and hope. He concludes by speaking once more to their life together as God's people (4:7–11).

In part 3 he puts their suffering into a theological context, while urging the elders to lead the others in properly Christian responses to undeserved suffering, as well as in their relationships to one another.

SPECIFIC ADVICE FOR READING I PETER

The special vocabulary of 1 Peter tells much of the story and should be watched for as you read. These words are especially important: suffering (11x); *anastrophē* ("way of life, behavior" 6x [1:15, 18; 2:12; 3:1, 2, 16]); God (39x); Christ (22x); Spirit/spiritual (8x); God's will (4x); election/calling (10x); save/salvation (6x); and hope (5x)—along with a number of other words that point to the future (inheritance, glory, etc.), plus a large vocabulary reminding them that they are God's people, living as "foreigners" or "strangers" or those in exile in the present world.

What propels the letter from beginning to end is their suffering. Peter's concern is that they understand their suffering in the larger context of God's saving purposes. Thus the strong emphasis on the work of the Triune God. God, the author of salvation, has both chosen and called them to be his people in the world. Suffering may therefore be understood as in keeping with God's higher purposes (his will); yet Christ's death and resurrection have made their final salvation altogether certain so that they live in hope. Note that Peter — significantly — always refers to Christ's redeeming work in terms of his suffering (rather than "dying") for us, which at the same time also serves as the example to be followed (2:21–24; 3:15–18) — all of which is enabled by the Spirit (1:2; 2:5; 4:14). All of this is said over and over again, with obvious interest in encouraging and reassuring them.

At the same time Peter is greatly concerned about the way they live, both their conduct as a people together and the way they respond to suffering. First, he repeatedly reminds them that they are a pilgrim people — strangers and foreigners here, whose inheritance is in heaven — and that they should live the life of heaven in their sojourn on earth. Second, by living in this way they will serve as God's priestly people for the sake of the pagans who are hostile to them so that they "may be won over" (3:1). Thus his readers are to fulfill their calling where Israel failed — to be a blessing to the nations. In the end there is not a thing in this letter that does not have these ends in mind. Be looking for them as you read.

You also need to have a sense of the first-century household in order to appreciate what is urged in 2:18–3:7. In ways that are hardly understandable to Western cultures over the past several centuries, in the first-century Greco-Roman household the male head of the house was the absolute "lord and master." In most such households, if he cared at all for things religious (and religion was a part of their way of life, whether taken seriously or not), then it was customary for the entire household (wife, children, household slaves) to adopt the religion of the householder. Peter is speaking into this context, where some household slaves and wives have gotten out of line on this matter by becoming followers of Christ, whereas when he speaks in a secondary way to the husband in 3:7 he assumes that he and his household have all followed Christ.

A WALK THROUGH I PETER

☐ 1:1–2 *Salutation*

This salutation is theologically compact. Watch for Peter's emphases: their election, their being "strangers in the world," and the saving work of the Triune God.

☐ **1:3–12** *A Berakah (Blessing of God)*

In keeping with the Jewish imagery and emphasis throughout, Peter begins with a *berakah* ("blessed be God"; cf. Eph 1:3), first with an emphasis on their sure future (vv. 3–5) before turning to their sufferings (v. 6), which have refining value (v. 7), pointing again to the future, this time with focus on Christ (vv. 8–9). This end-time salvation brought through Christ was prophesied by, but not available to, the prophets—nor to angels (vv. 10–12). After reading this section through and identifying these characteristics, you may want to go back and read it again to get a sense of its majesty.

☐ **1:13–2:10** *The Call to Holy Living As God's People*

With emphasis on God's call and character (1:15–17) and Christ's redeeming work (vv. 18–21), Peter begins by reminding them that God's call was to a holy way of life, especially in their communal relationships (1:22–2:3). God's goal is a "spiritual house" (house of the Spirit = temple), where a holy people offer "spiritual sacrifices" (2:4–8). Note how he concludes (vv. 9–10): By using language from Exodus 19:5–6 and Hosea 1:9 and 2:23, he reassures these Gentile believers that they are the new-covenant continuation of the people of God.

☐ **2:11–3:7** *The Call Particularized in Various Pagan Settings*

After an opening exhortation to "live ... good lives among the pagans" (2:11–12), he urges them to submit "for the Lord's sake"—first, all of them toward the governing authorities (vv. 13–17) and, second, the Christian household slaves (the Greek word is very specific) to their pagan masters (2:18–25), especially when treated unjustly. Here he appeals to the suffering and redemptive work of Christ with all kinds of echoes from Isaiah 53:3–6 (you may wish to pause and read the Isaiah passage, and then look for the echoes in 1 Peter).

Finally, he appeals to Christian wives of pagan husbands (3:1–6)—these wives have very little to say in such a household, but their manner of life must reflect Christ—concluding (v. 7) with a brief word to Christian husbands about their relationship with their wives.

☐ **3:8–4:11** *The Call Generalized—in the Face of Hostility*

Next Peter generalizes, beginning again with communal relationships (3:8–12), before focusing on how to respond to undeserved suffering (vv.

13 – 17), appealing to Christ's suffering, his proclamation (of triumph) to "the imprisoned spirits" (probably fallen angels), and his resurrection (vv. 18 – 22).

Note that, as in 2:18 – 25, Christ's suffering again serves as a pattern, this time for putting sin behind them (4:1 – 6). The concluding exhortations (vv. 7 – 11) once more have to do with life together as God's people, set in the context of "the end" — with God's praise through Jesus Christ as the goal.

☐ **4:12 – 5:11** *Conclusion: Suffering, Hope, and Christian Conduct*

Addressing the issue of their suffering one final time, Peter now (4:12 – 19) puts it into theological perspective (God's sovereignty and their rejoicing over the privilege of participating in Christ's sufferings and thus bearing his name). With a variety of echoes from 2:24 – 25 (regarding Christ) and appealing to his own role, in 5:1 – 4 Peter urges the elders to lead the people by their example in these matters (a very important "therefore" is not translated in 5:1 in the TNIV) before appealing one final time to their communal life (v. 5) and to their suffering while they await the "eternal glory in Christ" (vv. 6 – 11).

☐ **5:12 – 14** *Final Greetings*

The letter concludes with a very brief note about its purpose, concise words of greeting, and a final wish of peace.

Since most of the New Testament books are concerned with how the people of God live in their relationships with one another, it is important to the biblical story to have one that focuses especially on our being like Christ (repeating his story, as it were) in our response to suffering that comes as a result of pagan hostility.

2 Peter

ORIENTING DATA FOR 2 PETER

- **Content:** a "farewell speech" sent as a letter, urging Christian growth and perseverance in light of some false teachers who both deny the second coming of Christ and live boldly in sin

- **Author:** the apostle Peter, although questioned both in the early church and by most New Testament scholars; possibly a disciple who wrote a kind of "testament of Peter" for the church

- **Date:** ca. A.D. 64 (if by Peter); later if by a disciple

- **Recipients:** an unknown but specific group of believers

- **Occasion:** a desire to establish the readers in their own faith and godly living, while warning them of the false teachers and their way of life

- **Emphases:** concern that God's people grow in and exhibit godliness; the sure judgment on the false teachers for their ungodly living; the certainty of the Lord's coming, despite the scoffing of the false teachers

OVERVIEW OF 2 PETER

The letter is in four parts that focus on godly living in light of the certainty of the Lord's coming, against the backdrop of those who deny the latter, with its concomitant judgments, and who thus live like pagans. Part 1 (1:3–11) is an exhortation to growth in godliness, thus confirming their "calling and election" (v. 10) so as to "receive a rich welcome into the eternal kingdom" (v. 11).

Part 2 (1:12–21) is Peter's testament about the "coming of our Lord Jesus Christ" (v. 16), an event that both the transfiguration (vv. 16–18), which Peter witnessed, and the reliable word of prophecy (vv. 19–21) argue for.

All of this is set (in part 3) in the context of the greed and licentiousness of the false teachers, whose condemnation is certain (2:1–22). The main thrust of this section is to reaffirm the certainty of divine judgment on those who reject God by rejecting holy living; thus several Old Testament examples are brought forward by way of illustration. You may want to read Jude 4–18 alongside this passage, since it reflects similar concerns and uses some of the same examples from the Old Testament and Jewish apocalyptic. These teachers "promise freedom" but are themselves "slaves of depravity" (2 Pet 2:19), who would finally have been better off never having followed Christ than to have followed and then rejected him (vv. 20–22).

The false teaching itself is exposed and argued against in 3:1–18 (part 4). Against those who deny the second coming (vv. 3–4) is the certainty of God's word, and thus the certainty of coming judgment, and a biblical view both of "time" and of God's patience (vv. 5–10); the conclusion urges readiness, in obvious contrast to the recklessness of the false teachers (vv. 11–18).

SPECIFIC ADVICE FOR READING 2 PETER

Watch for the two (interlocking) concerns that drive 2 Peter from beginning to end: (1) the false teachers as such and (2) their denial of the second coming of Christ. You will find the description of them in chapter 2 especially vivid. Besides their immorality (licentiousness, sexual immorality, disavowal of authority), note that they are especially scored for their greed (2:3, 14–15) and the exploitation of the unsuspecting and unstable (2:3, 14, 18–19). And the twin pictures of their rejection of Christ are especially graphic — a dog returning to its vomit, a washed sow returning to wallow in the mud (v. 22). Note also how those on the other side, who eagerly await the coming of our Lord, are exhorted to "holy and godly" living (3:11–12).

Regarding the certainty of the coming of Christ, which will include inevitable judgment on those who reject him by the way they live, be watching for the emphasis on the sure word of prophecy, both Old Testament and apostolic. This is the point of 1:16–18 and 1:19–21, where the transfiguration of Christ itself was a prophetic foretaste of the future, and where true prophecy is completely reliable. The coming of the "false prophets" is also prophesied (2:1), while the final exhortation (ch. 3) begins by reminding the readers once more of the sure word of the "holy prophets" and the "apostles," with emphasis on the reliability of God's word—that the same word that brought the created world into being is preserving it for the day of judgment.

A WALK THROUGH 2 PETER

☐ **1:1–2** *Salutation*

The salutation emphasizes both the "righteousness" that comes from God and the "knowledge" of God and of Jesus our Lord. You should make a mental note that these emphases go together and anticipate much that follows.

☐ **1:3–11** *The Themes Stated: Godliness and the Eternal Kingdom*

As you read this section, think about how it sets out the major concerns: (1) God's power is available for all that is necessary for "a godly life" (vv. 3–4); (2) growth in godliness must be intentional (vv. 5–7); (3) without these qualities of godliness one cannot be an effective believer (vv. 8–9); and (4) the readers are thus urged to "make every effort to confirm your calling and election" (v. 10), with entrance into the eternal kingdom in view (v. 11).

☐ **1:12–21** *Peter's Last Testament*

Note now how Peter's testament (vv. 12–15) leads to an affirmation of the coming of Jesus, which is assured first by the transfiguration, which Peter witnessed (vv. 16–18), and second by the reliable word of prophecy, which has its origin, not in human will, but in God through the Holy Spirit (vv. 19–21).

☐ **2:1–22** *The Indictment of the False Teachers*

Following the emphasis on the trustworthiness of the prophets is the prophetic word of Peter about the coming of the false teachers, whose evil purposes and final condemnation are asserted at the beginning (vv. 1–3). What follows is so full of striking language and images that you will need to watch carefully for its "logic." First, the judgment on the false teachers and the rescue of the righteous are contrasted by means of Old Testament examples (vv. 4–9), concluding (v. 10a) with the two specific reasons for their condemnation, namely, living for "the flesh" ("follow the corrupt desire of the sinful nature") and despising authority.

These reasons are then elaborated with a series of images (vv. 10b–18a) that concludes by condemning the false teachers for destroying others as well (vv. 18b–19). Finally (vv. 20–22), they are condemned for having turned their backs on Christ and returning to the "corruption of the world."

☐ **3:1–10** *The Nature of the False Teaching: Denial of the Lord's Coming*

This final section lies at the heart of things. It begins, you will notice, with another reference to prophecy, recalling now both the Old Testament prophets and the apostolic predictions about such false teachers (vv. 1–4). Their scoffing, based on the lack of past judgment (nothing has changed since creation!), is responded to first by a reminder of the certainty of God's sovereign word (vv. 5–7; note that creation began with water and ends in fire) and second by appealing to God's forbearance (vv. 8–10; note how v. 8 echoes the reliable word of Ps 90:4).

☐ **3:11–18** *Exhortation and Conclusion*

The preceding warnings against the false teaching are now applied to the readers' situation by way of warning and exhortation (vv. 11–15a); note that after the judgment by fire comes the new heaven and new earth prophesied by Isaiah (Isa 65:17). This is followed by an appeal to similar kinds of things said by Paul about patience and salvation (2 Pet 3:15b–16), suggesting that some of the false teaching came about by a distortion of Paul's teaching. The letter concludes on the note with which it began—a warning and an exhortation to grow in grace.

As Peter's last will and testament, 2 Peter is critical to the biblical story, declaring the certainty of the Lord's coming and thus pointing the way toward the final book in the story, the revelation Jesus gave to John.

1 John

ORIENTING DATA FOR 1 JOHN

- **Content:** a treatise that offers assurance to some specific believers, encouraging their loyalty to Christian faith and practice—in response to some false prophets who have left the community

- **Author:** the same author who wrote 2 and 3 John, who there calls himself "the elder"; a solid historical tradition equated him with the apostle John

- **Date:** unknown; probably toward the end of the first Christian century (late 80s, early 90s).

- **Recipients:** a Christian community (or communities) well known to the author (whom he calls "dear children" and "dear friends"; the false prophets defected "from us," 2:19); it has traditionally been thought to be located in or around Ephesus

- **Occasion:** the defection of the false prophets and their followers, who have called into question the orthodoxy—both teaching and practice—of those who have remained loyal to what goes back to "the beginning"

- **Emphases:** that Jesus who came in the flesh is the Son of God; that Jesus showed God's love for us through his incarnation and crucifixion; that true believers love one another as God loved them in Christ; that God's children do not habitually sin, but when we do sin, we receive forgiveness; that believers can have full confidence in the God who loves them; that by trusting in Christ we now have eternal life

OVERVIEW OF 1 JOHN

You can experience some real ambivalence in reading 1 John. On the one hand, John's writing style is very simple, with a very limited and basic vocabulary (so much so that this is usually the first book beginning Greek students learn to read). It also has a large number of memorable—as well as some profound—moments. On the other hand, you may experience real difficulty trying to follow John's train of thought. Not only is it hard at times to see how some ideas connect with others, but certain, obviously significant, themes are repeated several times along the way.

Although, like most of Paul's letters, the aim of 1 John is to persuade, it nonetheless does not come in the form of a letter (notice that there is no salutation or final greeting). Most likely this is because John is writing to communities where he has direct oversight. What he writes includes teaching that "you have heard from the beginning" (2:24) about "the Word of life" who "was from the beginning" (1:1; cf. 2:13).

The primary concerns are three: the Incarnation; love for the brothers and sisters, especially those in need; and the relationship between sin and being God's children. The first two of these are the more urgent and are expressed together in 3:23: "This is his command: to believe in the name of his Son, Jesus Christ, and to love one another."

The Incarnation is touched on in 1:1–4 and 2:20–25, then specifically taken up in 4:1–6 and 5:1–12. The saving significance of Christ's death—the ultimate expression of God's love for us—is tied directly to one's belief that he "came in the flesh."

The concern about believers' loving one another is spoken to in a preliminary way in 2:7–11, then specifically in 3:11–24 and 4:7–21. The obvious tie between these two themes is that God's love for us, which we in turn are to have for one another, is fully revealed in the Incarnation, when the Son of God died for us (see 2:5–6; 3:16; 4:8–12).

The concern about sin is tied to the theme "Who are the true children of God?" This issue is first taken up in 1:5–2:2; it is picked up again in 2:28–3:10 and forms the concluding matter in 5:13–21. God's true children do not continue to live in sin, but neither are they sinlessly perfect; what matters is whether their obedience expresses itself in love for the brothers and sisters. The true children of God have already been given eternal life (= entered into the life of God, and thus are tasting the life of the age to come).

SPECIFIC ADVICE FOR READING I JOHN

As you read, be especially on the lookout for what John says about the false prophets, since they are the key to everything. Note that they have recently left the community (2:19), but only after trying to lead the whole church astray (2:26; 3:7; 4:1). These prophets apparently considered their teaching to come from the Spirit (cf. 4:1), which is why John urges that the believers' own anointing of the Spirit is sufficient for them (2:20, 27; 3:24). Indeed, in a marvelous wordplay on the language of "anointing" (*chrisma*), he calls the false prophets "antichrists" (*antichristos* = against the Anointed One). There has been much speculation about who these false prophets are, or what heresy they represent, but in the end these things cannot be known for certain, except that they deny the Incarnation, fail to love those in need, and (perhaps) argue that they are sinless.

The wonder of this little treatise is how much John can say, and say so profoundly, while using a notably limited vocabulary. But it is the very repetition of words, plus the use of stark contrasts, that is so effective. His special vocabulary tells the whole story: To remain/continue/abide (24*x*) in the truth (9*x*) means to believe in (9*x*) or confess (5*x*) the Son (22*x*), to whom the Father (14*x*) and Spirit (8*x*) bear witness (12*x*); it means further to be born of God (10*x*), so as to walk (5*x*) in the light (6*x*), to hear (14*x*) and to know (40*x*) God, to keep (7*x*) the commandment (14*x*) to love (46*x*) the brothers and sisters (15*x*), and thus to have life (13*x*), which is from the beginning (8*x*), and finally to overcome (6*x*) the world. All of this is in contrast to the lie (7*x*), deceit (4*x*), denying Christ (3*x*), having a false spirit (4*x*), thus being antichrist (4*x*), walking in darkness (6*x*), hating (5*x*) one's brothers and sisters but loving the world (23*x*), thus being in sin (27*x*), which leads to death (6*x*).

In putting all of this together for the reading of 1 John, it may help you to think in terms of a musical composition rather than a Pauline argument. A prelude anticipates the first theme, then the next two main themes are struck, or at least hinted at, followed by an interlude and then another prelude—this time to the major theme of the false prophets and their denial of the Incarnation. With all the major themes now in place, John works them over two more times each, adding and clarifying as he builds with powerful crescendo to the finale.

A WALK THROUGH 1 JOHN

☐ **1:1–4**   *Prelude: The First Theme Struck*

Life is ours through the Word of life, whom the author (already emphasizing the reality of the Incarnation) and others "have seen with our eyes . . . and our hands have touched."

☐ **1:5 – 2:2   *Second Theme: On Sin and Forgiveness***

Note the two matters emphasized here — that walking in the light (and thus in the truth) means to be in Christian fellowship through Christ's continual purification of sin and that those who deny they sin do not walk in the light.

☐ **2:3 – 11   *Third Theme: On Love and Hatred***

Now you will find three matters emphasized: (1) Walking in truth (light) means to be obedient to Christ's commands; (2) his command is the old one — that we love one another; and (3) failure to love is to hate and thus to walk in darkness (by implication, thus to live in sin, despite denying that one sins).

☐ **2:12 – 14   *Interlude: Some Reasons for Writing***

Notice that all of the reasons given for writing are intended to reassure his readers that they are the true children of God: Their sins are forgiven; they know Christ and the Father; they are strong and have overcome the evil one.

☐ **2:15 – 17   *Prelude to the Warning: Do Not Love the World***

Love has to do with the brothers and sisters, not the things of the world. Note that this second prelude sets the stage not only for the warning that follows, but anticipates 4:1 – 6, where the "false prophets" are set squarely in the world.

☐ **2:18 – 27   *The Warning: On Denying the Son (First Theme Again)***

Here you find John's primary reason for writing. By their leaving, the deceivers have obviously shaken up those who remain loyal. Along with the emphasis on the Incarnation, everything you find here was written to reassure the first readers that they have the true anointing of the Spirit (but John does *not* mean that people with the Spirit do not need teaching!).

☐ **2:28 – 3:10   *Second Theme Repeated: On Sin and Being the Children of God***

As this theme is elaborated, you can now make better sense of 1:5 – 2:2. At issue is the relationship between sin and being God's children. John begins by assuring them that they are the latter, before dealing with the issue of sin. Since this immediately follows the defection of the false prophets, it seems very likely that they are teaching that the true children of God are sinless.

☐ **3:11–24** *Third Theme Repeated: On Love and Hatred*

Again, it is not accidental that the discussion of sin(lessness) is followed by the truest evidence of being God's children, namely, loving each other as Christ loved us; while the "sinless" ones in fact live in the worst kind of sin: Not loving the brothers and sisters is equal to hating them. Note especially how verses 16–18 reflect the heart of the gospel, while also echoing the heart of the law (Exod 22:21–27).

☐ **4:1–6** *First Theme Repeated: On Denying the Incarnation*

Now you are back to the first theme. Here in particular the major teaching of the false prophets is exposed. The clear evidence that they do not speak by the Spirit is their denial of Christ's incarnation; this is the "spirit" of the antichrist.

☐ **4:7–21** *Third Theme Wrapped Up, and Tied to the First*

In coming back to the theme of loving one another, John now ties it directly to God's love for us as manifested in Christ's incarnation; his death effected God's atonement for us. Combined with 5:6–8, this passage suggests most strongly that in denying the Incarnation, the false prophets are also denying the saving significance of the cross.

☐ **5:1–12** *First Theme Wrapped Up, Now Tied to the Third and Second*

The true children of God are those who believe that Jesus is the Messiah (including his incarnation and atonement). They are also those who love the other "children of God." Verses 6–8 give us the best hints about the heresy itself: The false teachers apparently believe something significant happened to Christ at his baptism (thus he came "by water") but that his death was not something God was involved in (John thus insists he came by water *and blood*). The true Spirit bears witness both to Christ's incarnation and his atonement. Those who believe this have eternal life.

☐ **5:13–21**   *The Finale: The Second Theme Tied to the First*

After some words of confidence based on their believing what has been said up to now, John returns to the theme on which it all began—the issue of sin and who are the true children of God, who thus have eternal life. They need to flee idolatry—a final stroke against the false prophets.

After working through 1 John in this way, you can now also better appreciate the special emphases in John's telling of the story of Christ in his Gospel; it should also make the reading of 2 John make good sense. The whole biblical story stands or falls on God's love being manifested by his entry into our world of flesh and blood and dying for us in order to redeem us.

2 John

ORIENTING DATA FOR 2 JOHN

- **Content:** "the elder" warns against false teachers who deny the incarnation of Christ
- **Author:** see 1 John
- **Date:** see 1 John
- **Recipients:** the "lady chosen by God" is either a single, local congregation or a woman who hosts a house church; "her children" are the members of the believing community
- **Occasion:** John is concerned that after the defection of the false prophets from his community, they might spread their teaching in another community of faith
- **Emphases:** see 1 John

OVERVIEW OF 2 JOHN

What happens today when someone is disfellowshipped from a local church? Most often they simply go down the street to another church, usually without accountability on the part of the leadership of either community—the one they left or the one that receives them. In the elder's situation there are no other churches down the street for them to go to. But since those who have been disfellowshipped are "prophets," they can be expected to go from town to town, bent on convincing others of their "insights." These churches need to be warned.

Thus 2 John, a sort of miniature 1 John, presses the latter's primary themes—love and the Incarnation. But while 1 John was written to assure the elder's own community that they, not the false prophets, walk in the truth, this letter warns a house church in another town that these deceivers are on the loose. Notice also that 2 John 10–11 anticipate the concern over hospitality that will be raised in 3 John. Indeed, 2 and 3 John should probably be read together in order to see the two sides to hospitality that will be discussed in 3 John.

SPECIFIC ADVICE FOR READING 2 JOHN

Second and 3 John are both the size of ordinary letters in the Greco-Roman world, written on a single sheet of papyrus. Note how both letters close with a notice about John's wanting to talk with the recipients "face to face" (which probably indicates that he was running out of space on his piece of paper).

Given its brevity, you should especially note significant repeated words, both *where* they occur and *how often*. In fact, you may wish to do this for yourself before you read further, using different colored pens for the different words.

Did you note in verses 1–6 the repetition of *truth* (5x), its companion *walk* (3x), the associated word *love* (5x), and love's companion *command(ment)* (4x)? In verses 7–11, "the truth" is now *the teaching* (3x), which has to do with "Jesus Christ as coming in the flesh" and thus with his being the true Son of the Father. Several words refer to those who reject this teaching: *deceivers* (2x), *antichrist, anyone, them,* etc. This exercise pretty well tells the story about this letter. For the teaching itself, review the comments on 1 John, pages 412–13.

A WALK THROUGH 2 JOHN

☐ 1–3

These verses form the address and greeting. Written to the "lady … and to her children," John's emphasis is on true believers (the writer, the lady and her children, and many others) as those who "know the truth." Note how the greeting (v. 3) anticipates both sections of the letter that follows ("Jesus Christ, the Father's Son" and "in truth and love").

☐ 4–6

These verses urge that "we love one another"; this is what it means to "walk in the truth" and thus "walk in obedience to [God's] commands."

☐ 7–11

These verses warn against the "many deceivers, who … have gone out into the world." The content of their deception is a denial of the

Incarnation; the content of the warning is for "the lady" to deny hospitality to such people, for "anyone who welcomes them shares in their wicked work."

☐ **12–13**

The urgency of this warning is made clear by the fact that this brief and hurried note must be written and sent off before the elder can find time to visit and say these things personally and at length.

As a miniature 1 John, this short letter reinforces the role of the Incarnation and of love in the biblical story.

3 John

ORIENTING DATA FOR 3 JOHN

- **Content:** to borrow the words of New Testament scholar Archibald M. Hunter, 3 John is all about "the Elder, who wrote it; Gaius, who received it; Diotrephes, who provoked it; and Demetrius, who carried it"

- **Author:** the same elder who wrote 2 John (see 1 John)

- **Date:** probably in the A.D. 90s

- **Recipient:** Gaius, a beloved friend of the elder who lives in another town; other believers are to be greeted by name (v. 14)

- **Occasion:** an earlier letter to the church had been scorned by Diotrephes, who also refused hospitality to the elder's friend(s) and disfellowshipped those who would do so; consequently John writes to Gaius, urging him to welcome Demetrius

- **Emphases:** the obligations of Christian hospitality, especially toward approved itinerant ministers

OVERVIEW OF 3 JOHN

This is the shortest letter in the New Testament and thus the shortest book in the Bible (it is twenty-five Greek words shorter than 2 John). Along with Philemon, it is a personal letter; unlike Philemon, it is a private letter as well.

At issue is Christian hospitality, as evidence that one is "walking in the truth." The recipient, Gaius, perhaps a convert of John (v. 4), is a dear friend (vv. 1, 2, 5, 11; "dear friend" translates the Greek word *agapētos,* "beloved"). Along with the truth of the gospel (vv. 3 – 4), Gaius and the elder share the practice of Christian hospitality toward approved itinerants (vv. 5 – 8, 11 – 12).

Sandwiched between Gaius's two responses of hospitality toward strangers is the opposite example of Diotrephes, who has a twofold problem: (1) He is self-assertive in terms of leadership in the church (KJV, "he loveth to have the preeminence"!), and (2) his way of asserting himself is to reject both a letter from the elder and the approved itinerants who were being commended to the church in that letter. In light of 1 and 2 John, one is tempted to see Diotrephes as also on the false teachers' side of things, although doctrinal issues as such are not mentioned in this case. But in light of 2 John 10–11, hospitality toward strangers is not automatic; they must be approved as those who walk in the truth.

SPECIFIC ADVICE FOR READING 3 JOHN

This letter may seem strange to a North American culture, where itinerant ministers are usually *invited* to the church and put up in motels or hotels. But in some ways you might find the original recipients' culture more to your liking. In the first century, hospitality toward strangers was considered a virtue, and accommodations were often linked to a temple or synagogue. This practice became heart and soul for the earliest Christians. Thus if you were on the move, you could expect to receive hospitality within a local church community anywhere in the known world, a fact that runs throughout the New Testament. We find it in Jesus' sending out the twelve and the seventy-two (Luke 9:4–5; 10:5–8); it is mentioned by Paul as an expression of love (Rom 12:13) and is urged as a form of Christian conduct in Hebrews 13:2. By the very nature of things, such hospitality was usually expected of a householder, who was also the leader of the church (1 Tim 3:2), but it could also be the responsibility of any others who had sizable households (1 Tim 5:10).

Together 2 and 3 John help us see how closely connected a householder, hospitality in her or his house, and the church that meets in the house were in the first-century church. Strangers who claimed to be bearers of the good news about Jesus Christ needed to have letters of commendation (such as 3 John is for Demetrius) in order to be given Christian hospitality in the home that housed a church community. But even when the itinerants were well known (e.g., Titus in 2 Cor 8:16–24), they often carried a letter of commendation from a leader known to the community to which they were going (see Acts 15:23–29; Rom 16:1–2; cf. 2 Cor 3:1–3, where Paul is miffed at the idea that he needed such a letter in Corinth).

This cultural phenomenon is crucial to your understanding of 3 John, as well as of 2 John 10–11. In the present case, such a letter from the elder had accompanied some whom he had sent to a church; but Diotrephes had rejected it, refused hospitality, and disfellowshipped those who would like to have shown it—exactly the position the elder himself took in 2 John 10–11, indicating that the touchstone of everything is the gospel of Christ.

A WALK THROUGH 3 JOHN

After the traditional salutation (vv. 1–2), note the following:

☐ **3–8**

These verses are about *Gaius, who received it,* commending him because of the good report about his faithful "walking in the truth" (vv. 3–4), in this case pointing especially to his faithfulness in showing hospitality to some strangers, who went out "for the sake of the Name" (vv. 5–8).

☐ **9–10**

These verses condemn *Diotrephes, who provoked it,* regarding this issue; at the same time there is also some tension over the elder's authority.

☐ **11–12**

These verses commend *Demetrius, who carried it,* urging that he be shown hospitality.

☐ **13–14**

These verses conclude with words about *the Elder, who wrote it.*

Although the smallest document in the New Testament, 3 John enhances the biblical story because of the role it plays in giving us insight into Christian community and hospitality.

Jude

ORIENTING DATA FOR JUDE

- **Content:** a pastoral letter of exhortation, full of strong warning against some false teachers who have "secretly slipped in" among them

- **Author:** Jude, who modestly describes himself as "the brother of James" (thus of Jesus), but does not consider himself an apostle (v. 17)

- **Date:** unknown; probably later in the first Christian century (after A.D. 70), since the apostolic "faith" seems to be well in place (vv. 3, 17)

- **Recipients:** unknown; probably a single congregation of predominantly Jewish Christians somewhere in Palestine who were well acquainted with both the Old Testament and Jewish apocalyptic literature

- **Occasion:** the threat posed by some itinerants who have turned grace into license and who have "wormed their way in" (NEB) to the church

- **Emphases:** the certain judgment on those who live carelessly and teach others to do so; the importance of holy living; God's love for and preservation of his faithful ones

OVERVIEW OF JUDE

Jude begins and ends on the note of God's call and preservation of his people (vv. 1–2; 24–25). The body of the letter is in two parts: Verses 3–19 warn against the false teachers; verses 20–23 offer exhortations to perseverance and advice on how to help those who have been influenced by the false teachers.

The warning against the false teachers is sandwiched between descriptions of their ungodly behavior (vv. 3–4, 17–19). The meat of the sandwich (vv. 5–16) is a midrash (a kind of Jewish commentary) on some Old Testament and Jewish apocalyptic passages similar to 2 Peter 2, which offer precedents both as to the lifestyle of and God's sure judgment on the false teachers.

SPECIFIC ADVICE FOR READING JUDE

You can hardly miss the fact that the false teachers are the crucial matter. Fortunately, enough is said about them that we can piece together a picture of sorts. They have been accepted within the community as Christians (v. 4) and participate in their love feasts (v. 12). Very likely they are itinerant "prophets" (well known to us from other early Christian sources like the *Didache*), described as dreamers (v. 8) who in fact "follow mere natural instincts and do not have the Spirit" (v. 19).

Their teaching appears to be some form of libertinism: They have perverted "the grace of our God into a license for immorality" (v. 4) and follow their own evil desires (vv. 16, 18) like "unreasoning animals" (v. 10). That they "pollute their own bodies" in the "very same way" as Sodom and Gomorrah ("sexual immorality and perversion," vv. 8, 7) probably points to at least one dimension of their license. They also "reject authority and heap abuse on celestial beings" (v. 8, the latter is an indication of a Jewish Christian milieu with its reverence for angels), being "grumblers and faultfinders" (v. 16) who would divide the community (v. 19).

The fact that such people are destined by biblical decree to come under God's judgment and Jude's obvious concern for those who have been influenced by them (v. 23) indicate the seriousness of the problem.

A WALK THROUGH JUDE

☐ **1–2** *Salutation*

You may wish to compare Jude's salutation with that of James; note that neither of the Lord's brothers capitalize on that relationship in order to write with authority; they are, rather, his "servants." The salutation itself emphasizes the believers' calling and security in God.

☐ **3–4** *The Cause of the Letter*

Here you find Jude's reason for writing and the initial description of the false teachers; their denial of Christ is probably in terms of how they live rather than a theological issue.

☐ 5–7 Three Warning Examples

Note how the three examples of God's judgment (Israelites in the desert; angels [from Jewish apocalyptic]; Sodom and Gomorrah) serve two purposes, namely, to warn the readers and to point to the certain judgment on the false teachers.

☐ 8–10 Second Description of the False Teachers

Here the emphasis is on the false teachers' rejection of authority so as to go their own licentious way. The example given is from a Jewish apocalyptic work, *The Assumption of Moses* (early first century A.D.).

☐ 11–16 Further Warning Examples

Observe how eloquent Jude is as he now describes the false teachers—first in terms of three Old Testament examples (v. 11), and then with four examples from everyday life and nature (vv. 12–13), emphasizing their inability to make good on promises and their instability.

After citing from another Jewish apocalyptic work, *1 Enoch* (second century B.C.), as to their certain judgment (vv. 14–15), Jude concludes with a final description of their ungodly lifestyle (v. 16).

☐ 17–19 The Apostolic Warning

Note that Jude's final indictment of the false teachers comes from apostolic prophecy.

☐ 20–23 A Call to Persevere and to Help Others

These concluding exhortations indicate Jude's concern for the believers themselves. He first offers advice on how to persevere (vv. 20–21) and then urges them to help those who have been influenced by the false teachers (vv. 22–23).

☐ 24–25 Benediction

The emphasis in this beloved benediction is on God's preserving his people; note especially how it responds to verse 21. It is our responsibility to "keep [ourselves] in God's love," but in the end it is God's to "keep [us] from stumbling and to present [us] ... without fault."

Although very brief and focused, this letter's role in the biblical story lies with its emphasis on the importance of holy living, as well as on our perseverance and God's preservation.

The Revelation

ORIENTING DATA FOR THE REVELATION

- **Content:** a Christian prophecy cast in apocalyptic style and imagery and finally put in letter form, dealing primarily with *tribulation* (suffering) and *salvation* for God's people and God's *wrath* (judgment) on the Roman Empire

- **Author:** a man named John (1:1, 4, 9), well known to the recipients, traditionally identified as the apostle, the son of Zebedee (Matt 10:2)

- **Date:** ca. A.D. 95 (according to Irenaeus [ca. 180])

- **Recipients:** churches in the Roman province of Asia, who show a mix of fidelity and internal weaknesses

- **Occasion:** the early Christians' refusal to participate in the cult of the emperor (who was acclaimed "lord" and "savior") was putting them on a collision course with the state; John saw prophetically that it would get worse before it got better and that the churches were poorly prepared for what was about to take place, so he writes both to warn and encourage them and to announce God's judgments against Rome

- **Emphases:** despite appearances to the contrary, God is in absolute control of history; although God's people are destined for suffering in the present, God's sure salvation belongs to them; God's judgment will come on those responsible for the church's suffering; in the end (Rev 21–22) God will restore what was lost or distorted at the beginning (Gen 1–3)

OVERVIEW OF THE REVELATION

The cult of the emperor flourished in the province of Asia more than elsewhere in the empire; the result was that by the end of the first Christian century, the church in all its weaknesses was headed for a showdown with the state in all its splendor and might. By the Spirit, John sees that the martyrdom of Antipas (2:13) and John's own exile (1:9) are but a small foretaste of the great havoc that the state will wreak on the church before it is all over (see 1:9; 2:10; 3:10; 6:9–11; 7:14; 12:11, 17).

As a Christian prophet, John also sees this conflict in the larger context of the holy war—the ultimate cosmic conflict between God (and his Christ) and Satan (see 12:1–9)—in which God wins eternal salvation for his people. The people's present role is to "triumph over [Satan] by the blood of the Lamb and by the word of their testimony,... not lov[ing] their lives so much as to shrink from death" (12:11). As God has already defeated the dragon through the death and resurrection of Christ (the Messiah is caught up to heaven, 12:5), so he will judge the state for her crimes against his people.

The book plays out these themes in a variety of ways. The earlier parts (chs. 1–6) set the stage for the unfolding drama, starting with a vision of the Risen Christ, who holds the keys to everything that follows (1:12–20), while letters to selective churches represent their varied strengths and weaknesses (chs. 2–3). These are followed by a vision of the Reigning Creator God and the Redeeming Lamb (chs. 4–5), to whom alone belong all wisdom, glory, and power and before whom all heaven and earth will bow. As John weeps because no one can be found to break the seals of the scroll (which is full of God's justice and righteous judgments), he is told that the "Lion of the tribe of Judah" (5:5; see Gen 49:9–10), the "Root of David" (Isa 11:1–2, 10), has "triumphed," but the only lion John sees is God's slain Lamb (echoing the Exodus Passover [and Isa 53:7]), who has redeemed people from all the nations. Such a Conqueror can set the drama in motion by breaking the seals (Rev 6), which offer a kind of "overture" (striking all the themes) for what follows (conquest, war, famine, death [first 4 seals]—followed by many martyrdoms [seal 5], to which God responds with judgment [seal 6]). It is especially important to note that, apart from his role in the final battle (19:11–21), the only way Christ appears from here on in the narrative is as the slain Lamb; this is how his followers are expected to triumph as well (12:11).

The two interlude visions (ch. 7)—of those whom God has "sealed" from his coming judgments, but pictured in battle formation for their role in the holy war, and eventually redeemed—are then followed by the opening of the seventh seal, which unfolds as the vision of the seven trumpets (chs. 8–9). These "judgments" echo the plagues of Egypt, and like those plagues, announce temporal (and partial) judgments against their present-day Pharaoh. But as with the Egyptian Pharaoh, the plagues do not lead to repentance (9:20–21). The interlude visions between the sixth and seventh trumpets (10:1–11:14) call on the church to prophesy and bear witness to Christ, even in the face of death, while also pronouncing the certain doom of the empire, and ending with a foretaste of the final glorious reign of God and of the Lamb (11:15–19).

The remaining visions (chs. 12–22) offer explanations for and apocalyptic descriptions of the final doom of the empire. Chapters 12–14 thus give the theological and historical reasons for both the suffering and the judgment. The doom of Rome itself is portrayed in the vision of the seven bowls (chs. 15–16), which echo the trumpet plagues—but now without opportunity to repent. The whole then concludes as the (original) "tale of two cities," represented by two women (the prostitute [Rome] and the bride of the Lamb), in which the city that represents enmity against God and his people is judged (chs. 17–18). This is set against the backdrop of God's final salvation and judgment (chs. 19–20) and of the final glory of the bride as the city of God, the new Jerusalem that comes down out of heaven (chs. 21–22).

SPECIFIC ADVICE FOR READING THE REVELATION

You may easily find yourself in the company of most contemporary Christians, for whom the Revelation is difficult to read, mostly because we are so unfamiliar with John's medium of communication—apocalyptic literature with its bizarre imagery. Thus, along with knowing about the historical context and the way John works out his overall design (noted above), two other items will greatly aid your reading of this marvelous book—(1) to take seriously John's own designation of his book as "the words of this prophecy" (1:3) and (2) to have some sense of how apocalyptic imagery works, even if many of the details remain a bit obscure.

By calling his work "the words of this prophecy," John is deliberately following in the train of the great prophets of the Old Testament, in several ways: (1) He speaks as one who knows himself to be under the inspiration of the Spirit (1:10; 2:7; etc.). (2) He positions himself between some recent past events and what is about to happen in the near future. (3) He sets all forms of earthly salvation and judgment against the backdrop of God's final end-time judgments (see *How to 1*, p. 201) so that the fall of Rome is to be seen not as the end itself but against the backdrop of the final events of the end.

And (4) most important for good reading, John sees everything in terms of the *fulfillment* of the Old Testament. He has over 250 specific echoes of or allusions to the Old Testament so that every significant moment in his "story" is imaged almost exclusively in Old Testament language. This begins with the picture of Christ (1:12–18, with its extraordinary collage from Dan 7:9; 10:6; Ezek 43:2; et al.), climaxing in Revelation 5:5–6, where the "Lion of the tribe of Judah" (Gen 49:9), the "Root of David" (Isa 11:1), turns out to be a slain Lamb (from the Passover and sacrificial system). The church is imaged in the language of Israel in every possible way, beginning in Revelation 1:6, with its echoes of Exodus 19:6; its sins are expressed in terms of Israel's failures (Balaam/Jezebel), and its redemption in Revelation 7 is pictured first as a remnant of the twelve tribes and second as a fulfillment of the Abrahamic covenant, thus including the nations. So also the judgment against Rome (e.g., 14:8; 18:1–24) is expressed in the language of the prophetic judgments against Babylon (Isa 13–14; 21:1–10; 47; Jer 50–51), so much so that Rome is simply called "Babylon." The climax of the fulfillment is found in Revelation 22:1–5, with its restoration of Eden and total overturning of the curse. It is hard to imagine a more fitting way for the biblical story to end!

About John's use of apocalyptic imagery, you need to be aware of the following (for more details, see *How to 1*, pp. 255–56): (1) The imagery of apocalyptic is primarily that of *fantasy* — a beast with seven heads and ten horns; a woman clothed with the sun. (2) John himself interprets the most important images (Christ, 1:17–18; the church, 1:20; Satan, 12:9; Rome, 17:9, 18), which give us our essential clues to the rest. (3) Some of his images are well known and fixed — a beast coming out of the sea represents a (usually evil) empire; an earthquake represents divine judgment — while others are fluid and are used to evoke feelings as well as mental pictures. (4) Visions are to be seen as wholes and not pressed regarding all of their details, that is, the details are part of the evocative nature of the imagery, but the *whole* vision is what counts.

If you keep these various matters in mind as you read, you should be able not only to make your way through the Revelation but begin to appreciate some of its utter majesty.

A WALK THROUGH THE REVELATION

Introduction: The Historical Setting (chs. 1–3)

□ **1:1–8** *Prologue*

Note how the prologue sets out the essential particulars: John has received a "revelation" (Greek, *apocalypsis*) from Christ about what is soon to take place, which he calls "the words of this prophecy," offering a blessing on the one who reads it aloud and on the hearers in the believing communities (1:1–3). He then casts his "revelation" in the form of a letter to the seven churches, with appropriate greetings and a doxology—to Christ!

□ **1:9–3:22** *The Historical Setting*

Here you are introduced to the three primary "dramatis personae" (John, Christ, the church). John situates himself in his exile as their fellow sufferer, before giving the details of his receiving the revelation (1:9–11); he will be present as the "I" who sees and hears all that follows. Then he portrays Christ as Lord of the church (1:12–16, using a collage of echoes from Dan 7:13; 10:5–6; Ezek 43:2) and Lord of history (Rev 1:17–20; note how language for God from Isa 48:12 is appropriated by the Risen Christ!).

Finally Christ addresses the seven churches (Rev 2–3), revealing his knowledge of their present situation, usually exhorting them in some way, while urging those with ears to hear what is said, and promising eschatological rewards to those who are victors in the coming strife. The conditions of the churches are a mixed bag (some strengths and some weaknesses). All is said in light of "the hour of trial that is going to come upon the whole world" (3:10).

Introductory Visions: The Scene in Heaven and on Earth (4:1–8:5)

□ **4:1–5:14** *A Vision of the Heavenly Throne*

Before the awful conditions on earth are unveiled, John is shown first the incomparable and eternal majesty of God the Creator (ch. 4). This is responded to by the vision of God's Lion, the slain Lamb, who through his death has triumphed over the dragon in the holy war (see ch. 12) and who, because of his redemptive work, is worshiped along with God and is deemed worthy to unveil God's righteous judgments (ch. 5).

Don't go too quickly past these visions; all the rest must be seen in their light. You may wish to read Ezekiel 1 and Isaiah 6:1–3 for the Old Testament background to much of what is said in Revelation 4, and Genesis 49:8–12 and Isaiah 11:1–11 for Revelation 5. What John is offering is the perspective of heaven (where there is constant praise and worship of God and the Lamb), from which his readers are to view the gruesome situation on earth. This is made clear by his including the opening of the seven seals (6:1–8:5) within the framework of this vision, as 6:1, 3, 5, 7, and 9 make clear.

☐ 6:1–8:5 *The Opening of the Seven Seals*

Although part of the preceding vision, the account of the seven seals also begins a series of three visions (seals, trumpets, bowls), all of which have the same structure—a series of four, a series of two, an interlude of two visions, and a seventh.

In this first vision, the four horsemen (adapted from Zech 1; 6) represent conquest, war, famine, and death (= the empire against God's people). The series of two (fifth and sixth seals) also prepares the way for the rest by asking the two key questions: (1) The martyrs cry out, "How long?" and are told it will get worse before it gets better (Rev 6:10–11), and (2) those receiving God's judgment cry out (echoing Mal 3:2), "Who can stand [the day of God's wrath]?" (Rev 6:17). Thus John is given an overall prelude of the judgments that follow.

The immediate reply to this last question is the interlude. The ones who can stand are those who are "sealed" by God (Rev 7:1–8) and the multitudes who have come out of the great suffering—the redeemed of the Lord (7:9–17). As you read, note that the picture of the people of God in 7:1–8 echoes Israel's encampment in battle formation in Numbers 2, thus anticipating their own role in the holy war. This in turn leads to the next picture of their final rest in the presence of God, which echoes Isaiah 25:8; 48:10–13.

The opening of the seventh seal then marks the unveiling of the seven angels with trumpets (Rev 8:1–5). The silence is for effect; note that the judgments about to be revealed are in direct response to the prayers of the saints (6:10).

Preliminary (Temporal) Judgments on the Empire (8:6–11:19)

This first set of woes announces temporal, partial judgments while also anticipating the final one (chs. 16; 18). That is made clear by the fact that the first four are clear adaptations of the Egyptian plagues, which were temporal, not final judgments on Egypt, and the repeated motif of one-third.

☐ 8:6–9:21   The Judgments of the Seven Trumpets

Note how this series of four (8:6–13) picks up the picture of God's wrath from the sixth seal, but now as trumpets (warning judgments). Watch how John adapts three of the plagues against Egypt to fit Rome, who derives its power and wealth from the sea: hail (#7; Exod 9:13–35); river into blood, split into two parts—sea and freshwater (#1; Exod 7:14–24); darkness (#9; Exod 10:21–29).

The series of two woes (the third is withheld until Rev 18) pictures the judgments in more historical terms, feeding first on Roman fears of the barbarian hordes (9:1–12; men with long hair), but pictured in terms of Joel's locust plague (Joel 1:6; 2:1–5). This is represented second as a great and decisive battle (Rev 9:13–19). But even though the judgments are of temporal and partial nature, they do not lead to repentance (9:20–21).

☐ 10:1–11:19   The Two Interlude Visions

These two visions bring us back to John and the church. The first confirms John in his prophetic task (notice especially the echoes of Ezek 2:9–3:3 in Rev 10:9–11). But note that it begins with a mighty angel standing with one foot on the land and another on the sea, thus marking these off as belonging to God, not to Satan and his beasts (see 13:1, 11).

The second points to the prophetic role of the church, to carry out the expected end-time witness of Elijah and Moses (see 11:6), even though it means martyrdoms (vv. 7–10). But instead of the third woe (anticipated in 8:13; 9:12; 11:14), the seventh trumpet introduces an anticipatory picture of the end itself—but as already present: A song of triumph celebrates the consummation of the kingdom of God (11:15–19; note that the one "who was, and is, and is to come" [4:8] is now "the One who is and who was" [11:17]; what "is to come" is pictured has having come).

Conflict between the Church and the Evil Powers (12:1 – 14:20)

These three chapters form the absolute center of the book—not only literally in the overall design of the narrative, but as the theological perspective (ch. 12) and historical reasons (ch. 13) for everything, while chapter 14 prepares the way for the rest of the book.

□ 12:1 – 17   War in Heaven and Its Aftermath

Note how the two visions of chapter 12 offer the theological key to the book. In his coming and ascension (12:5, the whole story is recalled by picturing the beginning and end), Christ has defeated the dragon (pictured as war in heaven in vv. 7 – 11), who now goes off to wreak havoc on Christ's people.

Thus "salvation" has *already* come; Satan has already been cast down, so "rejoice, you heavens." But the end is *not yet,* so "woe to the earth." Knowing that his time is limited, Satan will pursue the Messiah's people (thus pointing to ch. 13), who will overcome him through Christ's death and their own bearing witness to it, even to the point of death.

□ 13:1 – 18   The Beasts out of the Sea and the Earth

This vision sets out the historical context for their suffering—prophesying how Satan will pursue them (economic restrictions and martyrdom)—which will take place because of their rejection of emperor worship.

The beast from the sea is an adaptation of Daniel's fourth beast from the sea (Dan 7:2, 7 – 8, 23 – 25). Pictured is Rome in all its apparently invincible might (note how in Rev 13:4 the people parody the Divine Warrior hymn from Exod 15:11) as it makes war against God's people (Rev 13:7)—which will lead to many martyrdoms (v. 10, echoing Jer 15:2). Note: the "fatal wound" that has been healed (Rev 13:3, 12) alludes to the year A.D. 69, when at the death of Nero the world expected Rome to collapse as it went through three emperors in succession. The fact that it didn't is what made it seem invincible.

The beast from the earth represents the priesthood of the emperor cult that flourished in the province of Asia. Note how those who do not bear the mark of the first beast (666 is a play on the name of Nero) are isolated economically.

☐ 14:1–20 *Outcome of the Holy War: Vindication and Judgment*

This series of visions then sets the stage for the final visions, picturing first the redeemed martyrs as firstfruits standing on eschatological Mount Zion (vv. 1–5), and then the fall of Rome in the language of Old Testament prophetic judgments—especially those against Babylon (which theme will be carried on to the end). The collection of brief vignettes (vv. 6–13) thus prepares the way for the rest of the book, as do the twin visions of harvesting the earth and trampling the winepress (vv. 14–20), which point to the future harvest of God's people and the judgment of Rome.

The Seven Bowls: God's Judgment against "Babylon" (15:1–16:21)

This third and final set of judgments (see chs. 6; 8–9) specifically singles out God's judgments against Rome.

☐ 15:1–8 *The Prelude*

Note how this prelude to the judgment starts with John back in heaven (cf. chs. 4–6), while the martyrs sing the song of Moses and the Lamb—an exquisite collage of passages from all over the Old Testament (see the TNIV note on 15:3–4). Note also how the setting (vv. 5–8) picks up the imagery from 11:19.

☐ 16:1–21 *Babylon Is Judged*

Watch how these woes echo the trumpets, but now without the "one-third" qualifier. As with the first four trumpets, the first four bowls are adaptations of the Egyptian plagues; note how the third one (water into blood) receives an immediate response in terms of the *lex talionis* (eye for eye). Here the set of two continues this motif. The interlude in this case (vv. 15–16) is noticeably brief and enigmatic (a call to readiness and a reference to Armageddon), while the final bowl of wrath repeats the earthquake from the sixth seal, at the same time continuing the plague motif (hail).

Wrap-Up: The (Original) Tale of Two Cities (17:1–22:21)

Using the powerful and evocative images of the two cities as two contrasting women—Rome as an opulent harlot; the church as the bride of Christ—John now places the judgment of Rome against the backdrop of

God's final judgments and salvation. Note especially how the two are introduced (17:3; 21:9–10) and concluded (19:9–10; 22:7–9) in similar fashion and that the one (the fall of Rome) is seen in the "desert" (17:3) and the other (the new Jerusalem) on a "mountain great and high" (21:10).

☐ 17:1–19:10 *God Judges the Harlot for Economic Oppression*

Note how this initial picture of Rome as an expensive prostitute sitting on the beast (ch. 17) echoes several such pictures of Tyre and Babylon in the prophets (Isa 23:15–18; Jer 51:6–7). Note also that the interpretations in Rev 17:9 and 17:18 make it clear who Babylon really is.

John then proceeds to sing a funeral dirge over her (18:1–3—talk about prophetic boldness!), followed by a call to God's people to escape from "Babylon" (18:4–8; cf. Isa 48:20; 52:11; Jer 51:45; etc.) and the resultant mourning by those who participated in her sins (the "kings of the earth" [provincial governors], merchants, merchant marine; Rev 18:9–24). Here at last is the third woe (see 8:12; 11:14), which itself takes the form of three woes (18:10, 16, 19). Here is the one place where John generally abandons the apocalyptic mode for a prophetic one, especially denouncing Rome's economic policies by which it grew enormously wealthy off the backs of the poor. Note how the immediate response to her doom is rejoicing in heaven (v. 20; cf. 12:12a), while another angel announces the finality of her doom (18:21–23) with echoes from Isaiah 25:10, ending once more on the ultimate reason for her doom—the killing of the martyrs (Rev 18:24).

And now watch as the threefold "Woe" is responded to with a threefold "Hallelujah" in heaven (19:1, 3, 6). And so John returns to the scene in heaven (from ch. 4), where the wedding supper of the Lamb and his bride, the church, is envisioned (19:1–10).

☐ 19:11–20:15 *The Last Battle*

The interlude between the "destiny" of the two cities brings conclusion to the theme of the holy war, both in John and in the Bible as a whole. This picture forms the final (eschatological) backdrop against which the judgment of Rome itself is to be understood. Christ is thus pictured as the Divine Warrior who takes on the beast, the prophet, and Satan himself (19:11–20:15); note especially how this "unholy trinity" is one by one thrown into the lake of fire (19:20; 20:10).

Observe how John pictures a separation between the final demise of the two beasts and that of Satan (20:7–10). This suggests, along with the scene in verses 1–6, where the martyrs are pictured as secure and presently reigning with Christ, that Satan still has a further time after the overthrow of Rome. The final event is the judgment of those who have followed him (vv. 11–15).

☐ **21:1–22:11** *The New Jerusalem: The Bride of the Lamb*

Structurally 21:1–8 belongs to the "last battle": note how it anticipates the city of God (described in the vision that begins in vv. 9–10), but also concludes (v. 8) with a note about those who have been judged in the "second death." Notice especially how it begins with language from Isaiah 65:17–19, with its "new heaven and new earth."

Thus John's final vision pictures the city of God, a new Jerusalem, coming down to earth, where there is a restoration of Eden and a reversal of the effects of the Fall (Rev 21:2–22:6). Watch for two things: (1) The city echoes language and ideas from Ezekiel's vision of the eschatological *temple*, where Yahweh's glory returns to the temple (Ezek 40:1–43:12), and (2) the city itself *is* the temple precisely because it is the place of God's own dwelling (Rev 21:3–4, 11, 22–23; 22:3–5). And note finally how much of 22:1–5 echoes Eden restored, also using imagery from Ezekiel 47:1–12.

☐ **22:12–21** *Epilogue*

You can recognize this as a true epilogue in the sense that it echoes many themes from the prologue. Thus, as a fitting conclusion to his vision that has taken the form of a letter, John both exhorts and invites his readers—and us—to participate in God's great future through the coming of Christ.

It is hard to imagine the biblical story ending in a more significant way. Here is the final wrap-up of the story, not only in the vision of the restored paradise in 22:1–5 but as the climax of the story of God's saving his people and of his judgment on those who reject him. John gathers up all the main strands from the Old Testament and places them in the context of the New, with Christ and his salvation of God's people as the centerpiece of the whole.

Glossary of Terms

The following terms are used on a regular basis in this book. Because some of them reflect technical language (allowing us the economy of one word rather than many), we have tried to isolate most of this vocabulary (plus some other technical language referring to pagan deities) and explain it here.

acrostic: Poetry in which each new section or verse begins with a succeeding letter of the alphabet.

agonist(s): In literature the major character(s) in the plot who are involved in a contest or struggle.

anathema: Something or someone placed under God's curse—or the curse itself. Thus, *anathema* can refer to something that is to be avoided as especially ungodly or repugnant.

Asherah: A Canaanite mother-fertility goddess often worshiped by the Israelites when they fell into idolatry. She was regarded as the sex partner of Baal and was worshiped for her supposed power to make animals and crops fertile. Most references to her in the OT are to her idol, a large pole presumably bearing her likeness. Asherah and Ashtoreth (see below) were so similar in the belief system of Canaanite polytheism that they are sometimes referred to interchangeably (Judg 2:13, "served Baal and the Ashtoreths"; Judg 3:7, "served the Baals and the Asherahs").

Ashtoreth: A Canaanite mother-fertility goddess similar to and sometimes considered the same as Asherah (above). Because her name in Greek was *Astarte,* it is usually assumed that the Hebrew form of the name may be the result of scribes' using the vowels (o and e) from the Hebrew word for "shame" to give her name a distorted sound in the biblical text. In some localities, distinctions between Ashtoreth and Asherah were made; in others they apparently were not, since it was the habit of polytheistic syncretism often to blur or interchange the distinctions between gods, with every location free to do its own thing with regard to worship and theology.

Baal: The chief male Canaanite fertility god—or the idol that represented him. Baal was sometimes called "the cloud rider" by the Canaanites because they thought that he controlled the weather, especially the rain, which was the key to agricultural productivity.

canon (canonical): The official collection of books that make up the Bible (or one of its Testaments). A canonical writing is one that is part of the Bible. Works judged not canonical were those that were considered not to "fit" within Scripture. "Canonical" is sometimes used to refer to the *order* of the books within the canon.

chiasm (chiastic): A literary device that follows an AB BA pattern (e.g., "food for the stomach; the stomach for food") of any length (e.g., ABCDCBA), which served the purposes of memory in an oral culture (where most people could not read but had sharp memories for what they heard read to them). This may happen in sentences, paragraphs, or large sections of books. We sometimes use the language of "framing device" or "bookending" or "concentric pattern" to refer to this phenomenon when we are dealing with larger sections of text.

concentric: See chiastic

conflict stories: Stories in the Gospels in which someone presents a challenge to or a criticism of Jesus, and he uses the occasion to provide a moment of instruction.

covenant: A formal legal-contractual arrangement in which both parties have obligations and responsibilities to one another. In the great biblical covenants, God's obligation is blessing and mercy to those who keep covenant with him; the obligation of his people is obedience, especially the obedience as expressed in loving God and neighbor.

cycle: A story pattern or theme that is repeated for emphasis or effect.

Deuteronomic: Notably consistent with and/or actually based on the theology or vocabulary contained in the book of Deuteronomy.

Diaspora: A NT Greek term used to describe believing Jews living outside Palestine in ancient times—especially NT times, although its beginnings go back to the Babylonian exile (when the majority of exiles did not return to Judah) and the self-imposed exile in Egypt recorded in Jeremiah 41:16–45:5. Also called *the dispersion*. In Acts 15:21, James refers to the importance of the Diaspora for the spread of the gospel when he says, "For the law of Moses has been preached in every city from the earliest times...."

discourse: A relatively lengthy and formal speech or written communication on a subject or a group of related subjects.

disfellowship: To remove someone from membership, attendance, and social contact with other believers in a church in order to correct a serious sin and restore the sinner. Such a severe action was undertaken because the sin endangered the church's own life and witness in the community.

Divine Warrior: A description of God in his role as the leader of the holy war (see below), a great fighter on behalf of his people (see, e.g., Exod 15:3; Isa 42:13; Jer 20:11).

doxology: A statement of praise to or about God, usually near or at the end of a biblical book or major portion thereof.

eschatological: Of or about the end times or last days, derived from the Greek word *eschaton,* which means "end."

exilic: Referring to the time during the Babylonian exile, which began in 586 B.C. and was officially over with the decree of Cyrus in 539 B.C.

fertility god: Any of the many Canaanite gods and goddesses, all of whom were seen as having the power to help people's crops and cattle be more fertile in exchange for being given food offerings. (Ancient pagan belief held that the one thing the gods couldn't do was to feed themselves!) See also *Baal* and *Asherah/Ashtoreth.*

Greeks: At a few points in the NT this term is used to refer to non-Hebrew (or Aramaic)-speaking Jews. Sometimes in Paul it also becomes a "stand-in" word for Gentiles.

Hellenists (Hellenistic): People who spoke Greek or followed Greek ways to some degree, even though they might otherwise be Jewish.

hermeneutics: Principles of interpretation, often used with reference to how biblical passages function for a later time and in new circumstances.

holy war: God's special battle against evil and those who manifest evil (very often in the form of idolatry)—a battle God fights on behalf of the righteous but allows his people to participate in. Because of God's omnipotence, there is no question who will ultimately win the war, but because of his great patience in waiting for evil people to turn to him, the war is not yet concluded.

horizontal: In OT law, describing the relationships and obligations of humans to each other; see *vertical.*

idolatry (idolatrous): A system that was inherently polytheistic, syncretistic, and (usually) pantheistic and that was present in virtually all ancient nonbiblical religions. Idolatrous practice relied on the belief that the gods could be influenced by offerings made in the presence of their idols, since the idols "manifested" the gods, including their nature and power; the idol was sometimes understood in both OT and NT to be the locus of demons or demonic power.

Incarnation (incarnate): God's becoming human in the person of Jesus of Nazareth.

messiahship: The position and/or action of fulfilling the OT expectations for God's special anointed servant-leader of Israel.

metanarrative: The great overall, overarching story of the Bible as a whole; the grand narrative of God's redemption of a people for himself, told progressively throughout the Bible.

monarchy: The period of time when Israel and/or Judah had a king, i.e., ca. 1050 B.C. – 586 B.C.

motif: An important idea or theme that constitutes one of the concerns of a book or passage.

oracle: A particular revelation from God; often used synonymously with "prophecy" or "revelation," when these refer to a *specific* message from God to a prophet.

panel: A distinct subsection of a narrative, containing a group of stories sharing a theme or topic.

passion: When used about Jesus, this refers specifically to his suffering and death.

Pharisaism (Pharisaic): The attitude that righteousness before God was related to obeying every OT law to the letter, including the Pharisees' own (often legalistic) extensions and extrapolations of those laws; and the attitude that only people who did so could be accepted as good Jews.

Pentateuch: The first five books of the Old Testament; also known as the "(Five) Books of Moses."

polytheism (polytheistic): The belief that there are many gods and goddesses, each with his or her own specialties and each potentially worthy of worship for what he or she could do better than any of the others. The whole ancient world was polytheistic except for those who kept covenant with Israel's God.

postexilic: The time after 539 B.C., i.e., after the Babylonian exile, which began in 586 B.C. and was officially over with the decree of Cyrus in 539.

preexilic: Before the Babylonian exile began, i.e., before 586 B.C.

Presence: God's special empowering manifestation of himself among humans whereby he gives a discernible sense of his greatness, holiness, support, approachability, etc. In OT times first the tabernacle and then the Jerusalem temple was especially often the locus of his Presence; in NT times it is primarily the Spirit in the church, but also in the individual.

proselyte: A Gentile who converted to Judaism and therefore practiced Jewish law, including especially circumcision, and was accepted into the Jewish community.

protagonist: The main character, main mover, or hero in a story or event.

restoration: The reestablishment of Israel as a people under God after the Babylonian exile.

refrain: A wording, topic, or idea that an author uses repeatedly for clarity or effect.

revelation: God's "unveiling" of himself so as to be "seen"/understood by people; sometimes used to refer to his imparting his truth to people.

sanctions: The part of the covenant that provided incentives to keep it, in the form of blessings (benefits from God) and curses (miseries of various sorts as punishments for disobedience).

sanctuary: A place where God specially manifests his Presence and where God is appropriately worshiped by his people.

Septuagint (septuagintal): The ancient Greek translation of the Old Testament, produced in the third and second centuries B.C. in Alexandria, Egypt. It was the Bible of most New Testament Christians, and it has had enormous influence, including on the order of the books in our English Bibles and in the NT sometimes on the wording itself.

Speculative Wisdom: The process of trying to think through what life and its choices really are all about. Asking and answering questions and responding to assertions—whether in dialogue or monologue format—are common in Speculative Wisdom literature.

syncretism (syncretistic): The sharing and blending of religious beliefs. When the Israelites continued to worship Yahweh as their national god but also worshiped Baal as a fertility God, or when they worshiped Yahweh via golden calf-idols, they were practicing syncretism.

theological (theology): Describing God, his truth, and his relationship to his world; also describing the particular way a given Bible writer conveys his part of the whole of God's truth.

theophany (theophanic): An appearance of God in some form. Although "no one has ever seen God" (1 John 4:12), God has "appeared" in the sense of specially manifesting his presence through angels (Judg 13:22), the incarnate Christ (John 1:18), storms (Ezek 1), etc.

tradition: Shared beliefs and/or practices passed on from one generation to another.

vertical: In OT law, describing the relationships and obligations of people to God; see *horizontal*.

vision: In prophetic literature, a special type of revelation in which what is seen helps orient the prophet to what will be said. What is described as "seen" in a vision is almost always simple, and normally it does not convey a message in itself, apart from the words of explanation that follow.

Appendix:
A Chronological Listing of the Biblical Books

This appendix is for those who might wish to read the biblical books in a chronological order. Some of this is guesswork, of course, especially in the case of the Old Testament works, since some books (e.g., Joel) are not easily dated. Our list is related primarily to their *content*, not to *date of composition* — although even in this case some exceptions are made: We have put 1–2 Chronicles before Malachi and Ezra-Nehemiah, and the Gospel of John with 1–3 John and the Revelation. Moreover, bear in mind that some books overlap each other in ways that a simple chronological listing cannot fully represent (e.g., Daniel and Ezekiel). The OT books that cover various times or contain few specific chronological clues have been grouped separately at the end of the OT list.

- ☐ Genesis
- ☐ Exodus
- ☐ Leviticus
- ☐ Numbers
- ☐ Deuteronomy
- ☐ Joshua
- ☐ Judges
- ☐ Ruth
- ☐ 1–2 Samuel
- ☐ 1–2 Kings
- ☐ Jonah
- ☐ Amos
- ☐ Hosea
- ☐ Isaiah
- ☐ Micah
- ☐ Zephaniah
- ☐ Nahum

- ☐ Habakkuk
- ☐ Joel
- ☐ Jeremiah
- ☐ Ezekiel
- ☐ Obadiah
- ☐ Lamentations
- ☐ Daniel
- ☐ Haggai
- ☐ Zechariah
- ☐ Esther
- ☐ 1–2 Chronicles
- ☐ Malachi
- ☐ Ezra- Nehemiah

- ☐ Job
- ☐ Proverbs
- ☐ Ecclesiastes

□ Song of Songs
□ Psalms

□ Mark
□ Matthew
□ Luke
□ Acts
□ 1 Thessalonians
□ 2 Thessalonians
□ James
□ 1 Corinthians
□ 2 Corinthians
□ Galatians
□ Romans
□ Colossians

□ Philemon
□ Ephesians
□ Philippians
□ 1 Timothy
□ Titus
□ 2 Timothy
□ 1 Peter
□ 2 Peter
□ Jude
□ Hebrews
□ 1 John
□ 2 John
□ Gospel of John
□ 3 John
□ The Revelation